D1467268

HEROIN

Other Books in the Drug Education Library series:

Alcohol
Cocaine and Crack
Hallucinogens
Marijuana
Nicotine

HEROIN

by Todd Howard

DRUG
EDUCATION
LIBRARY

LUCENT BOOKS
SAN DIEGO, CALIFORNIA

THOMSON

GALE

Detroit • New York • San Diego • San Francisco
Boston • New Haven, Conn. • Waterville, Maine
London • Munich

Library of Congress Cataloging-in-Publication Data

Howard, Todd, 1964–
  Heroin / by Todd Howard.
    p. cm. — (Drug education library)
  Includes bibliographical references and index.
  Summary: Discusses the history of heroin, its physiological
  and societal effects, and the extreme difficulty of fighting
  heroin abuse, both on an individual and a national basis.
  ISBN 1-59018-018-6 (hard : alk. paper)
  1. Heroin habit—Juvenile literature. 2. Heroin—
Physiological effect—Juvenile literature. 3. Heroin—
History—Juvenile literature. [1. Heroin. 2. Drug abuse.]
I. Title. II. Series.
  HV5822.H4 H69 2003
  362.29'3—dc21

                                      2001006808

Copyright 2003 by Lucent Books,
an imprint of The Gale Group
10911 Technology Place, San Diego, CA 92127
Printed in the U.S.A.

Contents

FOREWORD   6

INTRODUCTION
Heroin: An Enduring Problem   8

CHAPTER ONE
The Origins of Heroin   11

CHAPTER TWO
Heroin Abuse in the United States   29

CHAPTER THREE
Consequences of Heroin Addiction   44

CHAPTER FOUR
Preventing Heroin Abuse   58

CHAPTER FIVE
Recovering from Heroin Addiction   75

NOTES   89
APPENDIX: Warning Signs of Heroin Abuse   92
ORGANIZATIONS TO CONTACT   94
GLOSSARY   97
FOR FURTHER READING   99
WORKS CONSULTED   101
INDEX   105
PICTURE CREDITS   111
ABOUT THE AUTHOR   112

Foreword

The development of drugs and drug use in America is a cultural paradox. On the one hand, strong, potentially dangerous drugs provide people with relief from numerous physical and psychological ailments. Sedatives like Valium counter the effects of anxiety; steroids treat severe burns, anemia, and some forms of cancer; morphine provides quick pain relief. On the other hand, many drugs (sedatives, steroids, and morphine among them) are consistently misused or abused. Millions of Americans struggle each year with drug addictions that overpower their ability to think and act rationally. Researchers often link drug abuse to criminal activity, traffic accidents, domestic violence, and suicide.

These harmful effects seem obvious today. Newspaper articles, medical papers, and scientific studies have highlighted the myriad problems drugs and drug use can cause. Yet, there was a time when many of the drugs now known to be harmful were actually believed to be beneficial. Cocaine, for example, was once hailed as a great cure, used to treat everything from nausea and weakness to colds and asthma. Developed in Europe during the 1880s, cocaine spread quickly to the United States where manufacturers made it the primary ingredient in such everyday substances as cough medicines, lozenges, and tonics. Likewise, heroin, an opium derivative, became a popular painkiller during the late nineteenth century. Doctors and patients flocked to American drugstores to buy heroin, described as the optimal cure for even the worst coughs and chest pains.

As more people began using these drugs, though, doctors, legislators, and the public at large began to realize that they were more damaging than beneficial. After years of using heroin as a painkiller, for example, patients began asking their doctors for larger and stronger doses. Cocaine users reported dangerous side effects, including hallucinations and wild mood shifts. As a result, the U.S. government initiated more stringent regulation of many powerful and addictive drugs, and in some cases outlawed them entirely.

A drug's legal status is not always indicative of how dangerous it is, however. Some drugs known to have harmful effects can be purchased legally in the United States and elsewhere. Nicotine, a key ingredient in cigarettes, is known to be highly addictive. In an effort to meet their bodies' demands for nicotine, smokers expose themselves to lung cancer, emphysema, and other life-threatening conditions. Despite these risks, nicotine is legal almost everywhere.

Other drugs that cannot be purchased or sold legally are the subject of much debate regarding their effects on physical and mental health. Marijuana, sometimes described as a gateway drug that leads users to other drugs, cannot legally be used, grown, or sold in this country. However, some research suggests that marijuana is neither addictive nor a gateway drug and that it might actually benefit cancer and AIDS patients by reducing pain and encouraging failing appetites. Despite these findings and occasional legislative attempts to change the drug's status, marijuana remains illegal.

The Drug Education Library examines the paradox of drugs and drug use in America by focusing on some of the most commonly used and abused drugs or categories of drugs available today. By discussing objectively the many types of drugs, their intended purposes, their effects (both planned and unplanned), and the controversies surrounding them, the books in this series provide readers with an understanding of the complex role drugs and drug use play in American society. Informative sidebars, annotated bibliographies, and organizations to contact lists highlight the text and provide young readers with many opportunities for further discussion and research.

Introduction

Heroin: An Enduring Problem

During the nearly three decades that heroin was legal, hundreds of thousands of Americans from all walks of life who used the drug for pain relief and other medicinal purposes developed addictions to it. By the time the drug was made illegal in 1924, the majority of the nation's heroin addicts had relocated to the inner city to gain access to government-sponsored free-heroin clinics.

The majority of the nation's heroin use remained confined to the inner city for decades after the drug's illegalization. Because it was out of the view of mainstream America, society would come to underestimate the drug's potential for widespread addiction until epidemics of heroin use during the 1960s and 1990s showed the drug's alarming universal appeal.

Like the physicians of ancient societies, who believed that heroin's parent drug, opium, was a sacred panacea (cure-all) provided by the gods, American doctors once thought that heroin was a cure for ailments ranging from teething pains in children, to respiratory and stomach ailments, to alcoholism. The recent heroin epidemics have made it quite clear to the medical community, however, that the drug creates more illnesses than cures them.

8

Heroin's Impact

Heroin addicts suffer from a wide range of physical ailments, ranging from minor infections to organ failure. The all-consuming nature of heroin addiction can also lead to overwhelming psychological problems, which can culminate in suicide. Further, the emotional consequences of heroin addiction extend beyond the addicts themselves, to include an addict's family and friends. Also, heroin addiction negatively impacts society by causing increased spread of disease, addiction-related crime, and exorbitant emergency room and rehabilitative treatment costs.

Many experts agree on certain ideas about effective heroin abuse prevention, including the need to protect young people from the drug, as well as the need to prevent experimentation with other drugs that

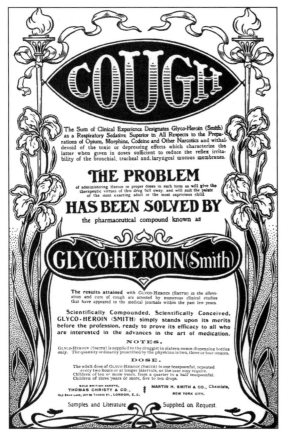

Before it was made illegal in 1924, heroin could be found in many over-the-counter drugs, such as this cough syrup.

are believed to lead to eventual heroin use. Experts disagree on far less than they agree upon, however, and opinions vary widely on what constitutes effective drug abuse prevention in general, and heroin abuse prevention in particular. As additional prevention approaches emerge, experts grow even more divided over how to best allocate the nation's very limited prevention resources.

If the past one hundred years are any indication, heroin abuse will continue to varying degrees in society into the foreseeable future. As some researchers seek effective prevention approaches, others seek effective methods for treating heroin addiction. Although experts may not concur about what constitutes the best method of treatment, they do agree that, regardless of the method, recovering from heroin addiction is a difficult, lifelong endeavor.

Chapter 1

The Origins of Heroin

Developed in the 1890s as a supposedly safe alternative to the opiate painkillers of the day, heroin was declared "a heroine in the war against pain" by its manufacturers, and aggressively marketed internationally. The arrival of such a drug was welcome news for a world that had for thousands of years relied on heroin's parent drug, opium, for pain relief and other medicinal purposes. However, opium had destructive properties as well. With the invention of heroin, it seemed that a miracle drug had finally been found that dramatically increased opium's pain-relieving and medicinal properties, while at the same time making its legacy of addiction, overdose, and unpleasant side effects a thing of the past. It soon became evident, however, that instead of alleviating the risks opium use had posed, heroin presented even more dangerous problems of its own.

The First Opium-Using Societies

Opium, a narcotic sap contained within the seedpod of the Asian opium poppy, has been used by humankind since the Stone Age. Since its earliest users had neither the knowledge nor the intricate tools needed to harvest the plant's sap, most of them probably obtained its effects by boiling, steeping, or soaking the plant's seedpods and then drinking the resulting tea. This seedpod tea probably delivered rather weak opium doses, however, since excessive amounts of seedpods and labor would have been required for potent batches. Thus, the drug's pain-relieving and other medicinal benefits, which include soothing respiratory and lower digestive tract ailments, would have been experienced at moderate levels by these earliest users. Likewise, its undesirable side effects, which include flushing and itching of the skin, dry mouth, and occasional nausea and vomiting, would also have been mild, and opium addiction and overdose was probably very uncommon.

The earliest known opium-users were the Sumerians in the highlands of what is now Turkey and Iraq. "The first reference to opium," explains pain relief expert Dr. J.C.D. Wells, "seems to have been an inscription carved on a tablet by members of the Sumerian tribe around 4000 years B.C."[1] The Sumerians were quite fond of the opium poppy, with its delicate white-to-pink or purple petals, and called it *hul gil*, which meant "joy plant." When the Sumerians migrated from the Middle East into lower Mesopotamia about 3500 B.C., they brought the opium poppy with them, and it became one of the main crops of the flourishing agricultural society that they developed there.

Sumerian poppy farmers in Mesopotamia discovered an even more efficient way to harvest opium. They found that if they cut incisions on the poppy's mature seedpod, which is about the size of a chicken egg, most of the opium would ooze out within twenty-four hours and dry into a latexlike substance that could then be scraped from the outside of the pod. This efficient harvesting technique, which opium poppy farmers employ to the present day, enabled people to eat or drink strong, concentrated doses of opium for the first time in history. The increased dosage strength provided the first significant medicinal pain remedy known to humankind, and led to substantially increased instances of opium addiction and lethal overdose.

The Sumerians passed their knowledge of opium harvesting to other Mesopotamian civilizations, such as Assyria. These poppy-culling practices continued from the Assyrians to the Babylonians, who would in turn pass their knowledge on to the Egyptians. About the time of King Tutankhamen's reign in 1400 B.C., the Egyptians themselves had become extremely productive cultivators of opium,

Making incisions on mature poppy seedpods extracts opium, the substance used in opiate drugs.

and the sprawling poppy fields of their capital city of Thebes had become internationally renowned.

Opium in Ancient Greece

At the end of the Bronze Age, about 1100 B.C., the Egyptians introduced opium to the ancient Greeks, and opium played a prominent role in their society until they were conquered by the Romans one thousand years later. The image of the poppy seedpod can be found in much of the art of the ancient Greeks, as well as on many of the coins and other artifacts from their society. As with most ancient opium-using societies, opium held supernatural connotations for the Greeks because of its seemingly miraculous pain-relieving properties,

The poet Homer refers to opium in ancient Greece's oldest surviving poem, The Illiad. *The Greeks revered opium for its seemingly miraculous pain-relieving properties.*

and much of their mythology contains references to the drug, including those of their oldest surviving poem, Homer's *Iliad*.

Opium also appears in the medical chronicles of ancient Greece, where it was praised by their earliest physicians, many of whom mistakenly assumed that it cured diseases because it removed the painful symptoms associated with them. The physician Hippocrates, for example, who is widely known as the father of medicine, praised opium's usefulness as a pain reliever and remedy for internal diseases, though he dismissed the widespread notion that it possessed magical attributes. Opium eventually received similarly high praise from some of the great physicians of the Roman Empire, including Galen, who prepared opium remedies for several Roman emperors.

Despite opium's powerful pain-relieving and euphoric properties, however, some ancient Roman physicians and scholars—most notably the well-known scholar Pliny the Elder—recognized its dangers and classified it as a poison, and considered it useful only for performing euthanasia on the terminally ill. They had seen opium cause crippling dependency and even lethal overdose in many of its users, and felt that its risks outweighed its medical benefits. In spite of such warnings, however, widespread opium use continued for the duration of the Roman Empire and made addicts of such historic figures as Marcus Aurelius, the emperor of Rome from A.D. 161 to 180.

Opium use spread throughout much of the world during the early centuries of the second millennium. Opium from the Egyptian fields at Thebes, for example, was introduced to Persia, India, and China by Arab traders, and its use was common in the Middle and Far East by A.D. 1000. High-profile opium casualties occurred in these places as well, including the accidental overdose death in 1037 of the great Arabic physician Avicenna. Avicenna had been an advocate of the healing power of opium during much of his lifetime, having praised it as "the most powerful of stupefacients." [2]

Roman scholar Pliny the Elder classified opium as a poison that should only be used for terminally ill patients.

Increasing the Strength of Opium

Despite opium's known dangers, people continued to seek ways of increasing its intoxicating properties for both medicinal and recreational uses as the centuries passed. During the 1500s, after traders and explorers brought tobacco and the tobacco pipe to Europe from the Caribbean, European opium users experimented with opium smoking, and found that it provided far stronger and more immediate effects than did either eating or drinking the drug. However, smoking increased the risk of overdose and addiction, as well as the severity of the drug's undesirable effects. Addiction to opium smoking quickly spread throughout Europe and the Middle East, and by the 1700s it had a tremendous impact in the Far East. Though the eating and drinking of opium had not been as popular

Inspired by the tobacco pipe introduced in the 1500's, European opium users began to smoke the drug out of pipes like the one pictured here.

The Opium War Between England and China

The Opium War is a particularly dark chapter in opium's long history. It began in 1839, after Chinese officials detained British opium smugglers who were employed by the British East India Company, and confiscated millions of dollars worth of illegal opium in an effort to curtail the staggering opium epidemic that was crippling China. The British East India Company had netted the British Crown a fortune during its four-decade monopoly on the illegal but highly lucrative opium trade in China. In response to Chinese efforts to end the trade, the British government declared war on China.

After the Chinese were overwhelmingly defeated by the British in 1842, the Treaty of Nanking, which the Chinese would call the "unequal treaty," forced them to permit England's opium trade in their country indefinitely, to give Hong Kong to Britain as a colony until July 1, 1997, and to pay for England's war expenses, as well as for the opium seizure that had touched off the war. China's opium epidemic continued into the early twentieth century.

in China as elsewhere, the practice of opium smoking for both recreational and medicinal purposes quickly caught on there (and would continue to cause addiction of truly epidemic proportions until 1949, when the Communist Revolution in China brought a halt to the country's opium trade).

Unlike their counterparts in the Middle East, European physicians and surgeons of the 1500s did not generally prescribe opium smoking to their patients. Potency among the batches of opium that were imported from the Middle East widely varied, making it impossible for Western physicians and surgeons to dispense safe and measured opium dosages through this method. Instead, they continued to dispense opium in the same way that had been used for centuries. They provided their patients with a moderately useful "sleeping sponge" soaked in water and opium. The sponge was placed on patients' tongues or over their nostrils for extended pain relief and surgical anesthesia.

In 1527, however, a Swiss physician and alchemist named Paracelsus created a more measurable (yet potent) form of medicinal opium than had previously been known. He dissolved a measured amount of powdered opium in wine and then added citrus juice and a trace of gold powder. Paracelsus found that opium retains far more of its potency when it is dissolved in alcohol than when it is in water. The resulting concoction, which he called "laudanum," either could be bottled as a tincture, or the black, gummy pulp that remained after the alcohol evaporated could be fashioned into pills of relatively uniform size and potency. He dubbed these pills "stones of immortality."

Though a very primitive surgical anesthetic by modern standards, laudanum was a breakthrough for sixteenth-century surgeons who were accustomed to operating on patients who were conscious and physically restrained. Modern-day anesthesiologist Michael A.E. Ramsay explains that before the advent of laudanum, "surgeons became very adept at performing fast operations. . . . 'Pitilessness' was expounded as an essential characteristic of a surgeon. Pain was considered a symptom of importance only in differential diagnosis, not as a problem related to surgical procedures."[3] Laudanum became the primary surgical anesthetic and pain reliever in European medicine, as well as the most common method of opium abuse in the West, for over three centuries.

Morphine Is Invented

Although opium had undergone increasingly effective methods of harnessing the drug's beneficial as well as destructive properties, a scientific discovery made in 1803 marked a turning point in the drug's history. Friedrich Sertuerner, a German scientist, discovered that dissolving opium in acid and then neutralizing it with ammonia isolated the drug's most intoxicating ingredient from the rest. Just as the ancient Sumerians had learned to isolate the poppy's sap from the rest of the plant, Sertuerner had found a way to further isolate the active ingredient of opium. This discovery made it possible to greatly increase the potential dosage strength of the drug. Sertuerner named this component "morphine," after Morpheus, the Greek god of dreams. To this day, morphine is believed to be by far the most intoxicating of the estimated fifty chemical components, called "alkaloids," that make up opium.

Morphine was immediately embraced by physicians as an important medical breakthrough, and was widely prescribed. This powdered drug, which patients took orally, not only provided stronger pain relief than that of raw opium, but its soothing effects on the respiratory and lower digestive tracts were considerably stronger as well. However, the most significant advantage of morphine over raw opium was that it allowed precise dosages. Though with morphine's increased potency came a proportional increase in addictiveness, physicians at the time considered morphine addiction a non-life-threatening vice that was well worth the drug's benefits. Morphine also produced stronger allergic reactions than opium, but doctors also considered these increased side effects to be worth the drug's medicinal benefits.

Developed in 1856, the hypodermic needle enabled physicians to inject morphine directly into the bloodstream. This allowed for more efficient and more potentially dangerous doses of the drug.

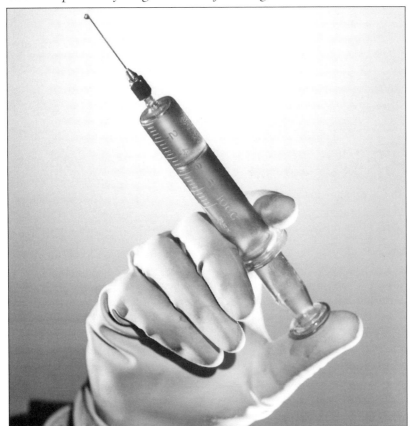

The power of morphine, and further, the overall quality of medical treatment in the nineteenth century, made a tremendous advance in 1856 with the advent of the hypodermic needle. Two American doctors first experimented with the use of the hypodermic needle to inject morphine directly into the bloodstream through a vein, and found that injected morphine yielded much stronger results in less time, and lasted much longer than morphine that was administered orally. Further, since the human liver does not destroy most of an injected dose of morphine, as it does with an oral dose, far less morphine is required for an injected dose. Sir William Osler, a distinguished British physician of his day, coined the widely used expression "God's own medicine" for morphine injections. This term reflected the common sentiment among physicians around the world concerning their newfound ability to bring extremely strong and rapid pain relief to patients for the first time in the history of medicine. Once again, the increased opiate dosage strength was accompanied by high addiction and opiate-related side effects, but as they had in the past, physicians considered these drawbacks to be greatly outweighed by the drug's power to relieve pain.

International Efforts to Regulate the Opiate Drug Industry

Widespread addiction to heroin was by no means limited to the United States; the drug was marketed throughout the world, and in numerous countries levels of addiction were comparable to those in the United States. Though concerns about the market-driven expansion of opiate drug abuse had existed in various countries before the marketing of heroin in 1896, the ravages of heroin addiction sparked an international effort during the early twentieth century to regulate the opiate drug industry. The Harrison Narcotic Act, passed in the United States in 1914, taxed the importation and sale of heroin and all opium drugs, restricted the amount of heroin or other opiates permitted in patented medicines, and required a doctor's prescription for the use of such drugs. Similar legislative reforms were implemented in dozens of countries around the world between 1909 and 1925. Most—but not all—of these countries also eventually decided that heroin had no legitimate medical uses, and made the drug's use illegal altogether.

Throughout the nineteenth century, raw opium was used in many nonprescription medicines, such as "Mrs. Winslow's Soothing Syrup."

Opiate Drug Use in the United States

At the time of the advent of the morphine injection in 1856, raw opium had already been widely used for medical and nonmedical purposes in the United States for well over a century. Both opium smoking and laudanum drinking had been popular among colonists before the Revolutionary War, and patented, nonprescription medicines containing raw opium had been available and widely used since the late 1700s. The use of raw opium did not subside with the advent of morphine injections and morphine-based nonprescription medicines. Instead, raw opium was featured in a growing number of patented nonprescription medicines, including such general remedies as "Dr. Barton's Brown Mixture," and "Dover's Powder," as well as the very popular "Mrs. Winslow's Soothing Syrup," for teething babies.

Various opium-based concoctions that promised to cure alcoholism were very popular, as were the many alcohol-based concoctions that promised to cure the opium addiction that resulted. In reality, however, many so-called remedies for opium addiction actually contained opium as a main ingredient—a fact that went unnoticed by users because the listing of product contents on labels was not yet required by

U.S. law. Also contributing to opium addiction in America during the last quarter of the century was the fact that laudanum drinking had become highly fashionable among men, and opium smoking had grown increasingly popular among women, since society considered alcohol use to be improper for them.

The Civil War had also contributed significantly to the widespread use of raw opium in the United States. Between 1861 and 1865, an estimated 10 million opium pills and an additional 2 million ounces of raw opiates were distributed to Union forces alone, with a roughly equivalent amount going to the Confederate forces. Consequently, thousands of wounded and traumatized soldiers from both sides began to suffer from opium addiction—a condition then referred to as "army disease" or "soldier's disease." Also, the war provided America with ample opportunity to use the new morphine injection, and it was highly effective in treating the pain and dysentery that were a constant on the battlefield. Off the battlefield, morphine injections were used as treatment for the opium withdrawal experienced by soldiers, as well as for the emotional trauma experienced by the families of disabled and killed soldiers. Of course, these treatments only served to compound the nation's growing opium problem, and addiction to injected morphine quickly rivaled that of raw opium. "After the war," author Charles F. Levinthal writes, "thousands of ex-soldiers continued to use [morphine] for these purposes, and they recommended it to friends and relatives. The United States Pension Bureau had difficulties with large numbers of veterans suffering from the 'army disease' . . . until well into the twentieth century."[4]

Predictably, the demand for patented medicines containing morphine rose after the war, and physicians recommended these medicines not only to veterans of the war, but also to the general public as a cure-all for the wide variety of ailments for which there were not yet legitimate medical treatments. "A popular medical textbook in 1880 listed fifty-four diseases that could be treated with morphine injections," notes Levinthal, "ranging from anemia and angina pectoris through diabetes, nymphomania, and ovarian neuralgia, to tetanus, vaginismus, and morning sickness."[5]

Not all doctors sanctioned the use of morphine as a panacea, however, including John Witherspoon, a noted physician who eventually became the president of the American Medical Association. "Ah, Brothers!" Witherspoon cautions his colleagues, "we, the representatives of the grandest and noblest profession in the world . . . must . . . warn and save our people from the clutches of this hydra-headed monster. . . . The morphine habit is growing at an alarming rate, and we can not shift the responsibility, but must acknowledge that we are culpable in too often giving this seductive siren until the will power is gone."[6]

Diacetylmorphine (Heroin) Is Invented

By the 1890s, the various forms of opium and morphine use had led to very real addiction problems in the United States and abroad, and it became evident to the international medical community that something had to be done about it. "Finally recognizing the seriousness of the addiction problem," explains author Alfred W. McCoy, "medical science devoted considerable pharmacological research to finding a non-addicting pain killer."[7] Aware of the tremendous market for such a drug, Bayer Pharmaceutical Company of Germany embarked on its own large-scale research program. One of Bayer's research chemists, Heinrich Dreser, recalled having read about a drug that

This early Bayer advertisement indicates the arrival of both heroin and aspirin in the pharmaceutical marketplace.

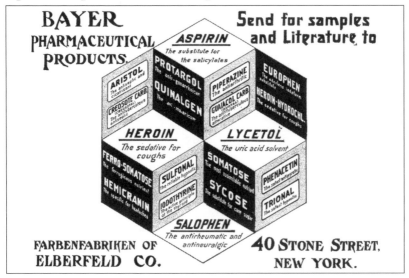

had been invented twenty years before by C.R. Wright, a researcher in England. Wright, he recalled, had found that boiling morphine and a common industrial acid called acetic anhydride together over a stove for several hours produced a drug that was at least ten times more powerful than ordinary medical morphine, and that it reached the brain far more quickly as well. Wright had concluded, however, that the resulting drug, which he named "diacetylmorphine," possessed too many negative effects to be a practical painkiller, and he discontinued his experiments with it.

With the race heating up among major pharmaceutical companies to find a nonaddictive opiate drug, Dreser, who also invented aspirin for Bayer, decided to reevaluate Wright's conclusions about diacetylmorphine. Upon tinkering with Wright's recipe, Dreser created a form of diacetylmorphine that upon injection, was immediately metabolized by the body into a morphine dose approximately twenty-five times stronger than a morphine injection of the same size. Further, Dreser and his research team found that since less of this powerful diacetylmorphine was needed, fewer of opium's undesirable allergen-related side effects were caused. Based on these encouraging results, Dreser assumed that diacetylmorphine was also largely free of the addictive properties present in other opiate drugs, and thus, that diacetylmorphine would enable opiate drug addicts to break their addiction by simply switching to it for a brief time and then discontinuing its use whenever they chose to.

The Marketing of Heroin

Dreser felt that his new drug was not only nonaddictive but also an effective treatment for respiratory illnesses such as bronchitis, chronic coughing, asthma, and tuberculosis. However, other researchers at Bayer disagreed. These skeptics suspected that diacetylmorphine, and all opiate drugs, have a depressant effect on the central nervous system and the respiratory system, thereby slowing and lessening the body's breathing impulse. Although diacetylmorphine seemed to improve respiratory conditions, they suggested, it merely suppressed the body's urge to cough—a masking of symptoms.

Details of Poppy Growing

Opium poppies grow from a very small, round seed to reach a height of between two and five feet. In less than six weeks the young plant has grown four large leaves and resembles a small cabbage in appearance. The plant then flowers, and its four petals can be white, pink, reddish purple, or crimson red in color. The petals last for two to four days and then drop to reveal a small, round, green seedpod, which continues to grow until it is about the size of a chicken egg. The plant's opium sap is produced within the walls of the seedpod, and it secretes more than 95 percent of its opium when it is scored with a knife. The entire growth cycle for opium poppies is about 120 days, during which the plant flowers and bears seedpods only once.

Despite the doubts of some of its chemists, Bayer deferred to Dreser's optimistic assessment of diacetylmorphine, and announced to the world in 1898 that it had invented a revolutionary new drug that was a nonaddictive painkiller and cure for opium and morphine addiction, as well as an effective treatment for all breathing ailments and a soother of digestive disorders. They chose the brand name "heroin" for diacetylmorphine, and launched an aggressive international advertising campaign in a dozen different languages, touting the drug as "a heroine in the war against pain." Heroin, like morphine before it, and opium before morphine, was hailed as a miracle drug by physicians, and was widely prescribed as a nonaddictive cure for practically every ailment.

One of those many ailments was addiction to morphine. Physicians quickly administered heroin injections to intravenous (in the vein) morphine addicts, expecting it would soon free these patients from their crippling addictions. The philanthropic Saint James Society launched a campaign in which free heroin was supplied through the mail to morphine addicts who were trying to give up their habits. Bayer also marketed heroin as an over-the-counter drug, and it soon became one of the most popular patented medicines of any sort on the market. Since there were an estimated 1 million opiate drug addicts in America by 1900, heroin was big business as these users switched to this new drug en masse. Heroin's popularity was a worldwide phenomenon; between 1899 and 1913, Bayer exported over one ton of the drug annually to over twenty-three countries.

The Impact of Heroin

There was no immediate evidence that heroin could successfully treat respiratory ailments, since patients with terminal respiratory illnesses, such as tuberculosis, continued to die in spite of their heroin treatments. Heroin did seem to be a truly superior cough suppressant for these patients, however, and thereby enabled them to die without the tortuous coughing and pain that they would otherwise have experienced. The debate over whether heroin provided legitimate treatment for respiratory ailments, or simply depressed respiratory functions, continued for a full decade after the drug's introduction into the marketplace, and spawned over 180 clinical studies and reports on its use in over ten thousand patients. By 1910, the evidence had overwhelm-

Opiate drugs were used in cough suppressants like "Dr. Seth Arnold's Cough Killer" because opium depresses respiratory functions.

ingly demonstrated that heroin merely had a depressant effect on the respiratory system. Dreser, like his predecessors in ancient opium-using societies, had naively assumed that since the drug removed the symptoms of diseases, it therefore cured them.

Though the vast majority of the medical studies conducted during the first decade of heroin's legal use were focused on the drug's effects on the respiratory system, additional questions arose within the medical community concerning the claim that the drug was nonaddictive. Patients across the country reported experiencing withdrawal symptoms, including violent muscular aches and spasms, chills, and sweating, that were worse than those encountered with serious morphine addiction. By 1903 medical journals were rightly suggesting that heroin's uniqueness lay not only in the degree to which it killed pain, but also in the degree to which it created crippling physical dependency.

The addictiveness of heroin became obvious as reports of addiction continued to mount at an alarming rate between 1903 and 1906. By 1906 the medical community had reached the overwhelming consensus that heroin was at least twice as addictive as morphine. The U.S. government responded to pressure from the medical community by passing the 1906 Pure Food and Drug Act, which required warnings of the potential for addiction on the labels of all opiate products.

Despite the continuing concerns of both the medical and law enforcement communities regarding both heroin and the other opiates present in society, however, the U.S. government was slow to take further action. Though in 1914 Congress did pass the Harrison Act, which required a prescription for heroin use, set limits on the amount of heroin permitted in patented preparations, and taxed the sale and manufacture of heroin, it did not pass legislation outlawing the importation, manufacture, sale, and use of heroin until 1924.

The immediate impact of heroin use in the United States was a fiercer addiction for hundreds of thousands of already suffering addicts, as well as the creation of many new addicts. The long-term result has been the permanent presence in society of an intensely addictive and deadly opiate drug that continues to inflict tremendous suffering on its many users and, by association, their friends, families, and communities. Some medical experts today do still consider heroin to have a narrow range of legitimate and unique medical uses—most notably its ability to comfort the terminally ill with its unmatched pain-relieving powers. However, there is little argument that the consequences of heroin use for other medical purposes have far outweighed its benefits—that the drug has fallen well short of its intended role as a "heroine in the war against pain." Rather, by pushing opium's powers of destruction to their ultimate extreme, heroin can be said to have played something more akin to the role of saboteur in such a war.

Chapter 2

Heroin Abuse in the United States

During the three decades that heroin use was legal in America, heroin abuse occurred throughout the country and affected people of both sexes and of all social classes and races. When heroin was made illegal in 1924, however, abuse of the drug became most prevalent in the inner cities. As a result, heroin abuse faded from the view of mainstream America, and addiction stopped being considered a problem that could affect nearly anyone. Instead, the drug would come to be dismissed by most Americans as something that could affect only the inner-city poor.

However, during the 1960s and again in the 1990s, heroin abuse rose among the wealthy and the middle class. Heroin's renewed widespread popularity served as a reminder to American society that heroin abuse is a problem that does not discriminate along lines of socioeconomic standing, race, or age.

Heroin Moves to the Inner City

The relocation of most of the nation's heroin addicts into the American inner city during the 1920s was the result of a well-meaning, if ill-conceived government program that dispensed free heroin from medical clinics in these densely populated places. The majority of the nation's approximately 200,000 heroin addicts flocked to the big

A detective at the New York Police Department's Bureau of Narcotics in 1939 works to enforce drug laws that illegalized heroin in 1924.

cities to gain daily access to these clinics. During the five years that preceded Congress's decision to make heroin illegal in 1924, addicts who registered at these clinics received daily heroin dosages, with the strength of their daily dosage being gradually decreased over time in an effort to wean them off of the drug. This program did not serve to reduce the number of addicts, however, but instead served only to compound the nation's heroin problem in a variety of ways. Not only did these efforts to cure existing addiction fail miserably, but, as the U.S. Drug Enforcement Administration notes, people who were not already addicted to the drug began to show up to get it, and "statistics showed that these clinics actually raised the number of addicts."[8] Further, since the forced closure of these clinics in 1924 left inner-city addicts needing nearly every dime for the purchase of heroin, they stood little chance of getting out of these places.

After heroin was made illegal, all that most Americans came to know of the drug and its users was what they read in the evening news. They read of the crimes committed in the inner city by addicts who needed money to purchase the drug, of the rising percentage of the nation's prison population that was serving sentences for such crimes, and of the even higher percentage of the nation's prison population (a full one-third by 1928) that was serving sentences for possession of the drug.

With the disappearance of heroin clinics in 1924, the demand for heroin was met by individuals and small-scale criminal organizations. When international political pressure tightened controls on the manufacture and sale of European pharmaceutical heroin, however, black-market (illegally manufactured and sold) heroin became increasingly difficult for these small-time smugglers and dealers to obtain. As a result, the purity of street heroin in the United States was quite low and the price was high.

The U.S. heroin trade underwent a dramatic and permanent transformation during the early 1930s, however, when gangster Salvatore C. Luciano, known to the world as "Lucky" Luciano, became the

During the early 1930's, the Italian Mafia, under the leadership of Salvatore "Lucky" Luciano, took control of the lucrative business of heroin trafficking in the U.S.

head of the Mafia. Under Luciano, the Mafia entered and soon dominated the lucrative markets of heroin and prostitution, and instituted an integrated system of smuggling, promotion, and sale of the drug in major cities around the country. The Mafia soon found that heroin dealing and prostitution complemented one another, since heroin-addicted prostitutes were virtually guaranteed to remain in the servitude of an employer that had an endless supply of the drug. The fact that many prostitutes were now heroin addicts, and were associated with the Mafia, helped to foster the assumption of many Americans that heroin could hold appeal only to immoral, inner-city criminals.

The Mafia became part of a sophisticated, international crime syndicate that had begun manufacturing and trafficking heroin in response to the disappearance of European pharmaceutical heroin from the black market. The majority of the heroin smuggled into the United States originated in the poppy fields of the "Golden Triangle" countries of Laos, Thailand, and Burma, and was processed in clandestine laboratories in Shanghai and Tientsin, China. "Owned and operated by a powerful Chinese secret society," explains author Alfred

Much of the heroin smuggled into the United States was grown in the poppy fields of Laos, Thailand, and Burma, called the "Golden Triangle."

The French Connection

Following World War II, as the international heroin trade resumed, a number of heroin refineries appeared in Marseilles, France. These refineries, which have come to be known as "the French Connection," were run by a Mafia family known as the Lucchese crime syndicate. The refineries processed opium from the Middle East, and supplied a tremendous amount of heroin to the rapidly expanding U.S. black market for nearly two decades. In 1961, however, the Lucchese family was indicted in what was then the largest heroin-smuggling case ever in the United States, after New York police seized a car that had been shipped to the United States from France, and which had $32 million worth of the drug hidden within it.

Though the interception of this smuggled heroin resulted in the convictions of a number of high-ranking members of the Mafia family, a strange twist in this case occurred a decade later when the seized heroin was stolen from the closely guarded evidence storage facilities of the New York Police Department, and presumably, sold on the streets of the United States after all. The resulting investigation revealed that the theft had been a joint effort of the Lucchese crime family and corrupt U.S. officials.

Thomas "Three Finger Brown" Lucchese was the first witness to appear before the Senate regarding his family's involvement with the Mafia and heroin trafficking.

W. McCoy, "these laboratories started to supply vast quantities of illicit heroin to corrupt Chinese warlords, European criminal syndicates, and American mafiosi like Lucky Luciano."[9] Additional heroin came to the United States from laboratories in Marseilles, France, where newly formed criminal organizations processed opium grown in the "Golden Crescent" countries of Iran, Afghanistan, and Pakistan.

The Great Depression and World War II

With these established smuggling pipelines and a comprehensive heroin distribution system in place in American cities, dealers began doing a brisk heroin business in the early 1930s. They likely would have expanded their sales substantially throughout the decade if the Great Depression—a worldwide economic slump—hadn't interrupted their plans. The economic hardship of the depression postponed further spread of heroin use in the inner city, since money for the purchase of the drug was largely unobtainable by any means. Further, World War II brought international drug traffic to a complete halt. McCoy explains:

> Wartime border security measures and a shortage of ordinary commercial shipping made it nearly impossible for traffickers to smuggle heroin into the United States. Distributors augmented dwindling supplies by "cutting" [mixing] heroin with increasingly greater proportions of sugar or quinine; while most packets of heroin sold in the United States [in 1938] were 28 percent pure, only three years later they were less than 3 percent pure. As a result of all this, many American addicts were forced to undergo involuntary withdrawal from their habits, and by the end of World War II the American addict population had dropped to less than twenty thousand. In fact, as the war drew to a close, there was every reason to believe that the scourge of heroin had finally been purged from the United States.[10]

By the time the war ended in 1945, consumer demand for the drug was the lowest it had been in fifty years. Supplies were nonexistent, and international criminal syndicates had fallen into disarray.

Within several years, however, criminal syndicates had regrouped, the poppy fields had begun to flourish once again in Southeast Asia, and new heroin refineries began to appear both in Marseilles and Hong Kong. In the United States, the heroin trade quickly and quietly resumed as the Mafia, still led by Lucky Luciano, flooded the American inner city with inexpensive, high-purity heroin. Despite their forced withdrawal during the war, America's addicts quickly resumed their use of the drug, and the estimated twenty-thousand active addicts at the war's close in 1945 nearly tripled by the decade's end.

This abundance of heroin in the streets of the destitute inner city after the war also created new addicts among the influx of primarily minority and immigrant workers who had flooded there in search of employment during the war. Author Jara A. Krivanek notes that heroin was introduced by longtime users to the African-American and Puerto Rican communities who had come to the cities looking for work:

> Like all new immigrants, they worked at the lowest economic levels, settled in slum neighborhoods, and endured unemployment, poverty and discrimination. From 1947 to 1951 the use of heroin spread steadily among these and other lower class, slum-dwelling people. . . . The increase was gradual, and did not attract much attention. Most of the users were in their twenties and thirties.[11]

Criminal syndicates regrouped after World War II, and heroin was once again smuggled into the United States from places like Hong Kong (pictured).

By the mid-1950s, heroin abuse began to spread to the teenagers of the inner city and was particularly popular among street gangs. Unlike many of the drug's older users, whose wartime jobs had provided them with the skills needed to obtain gainful employment after the war, these teens relied for the most part on crime to support their habits. As a result, the crime rate and associated arrests in the inner city began to rise, and the nation's assumptions that the drug could affect only the inner-city poor were further reinforced.

The Heroin Epidemic of the 1960s

During the 1960s, however, these long-standing misconceptions about the potential scope of heroin's appeal were rocked as heroin and other drugs gained popularity among middle-class teens. These teens, many of whom were involved in the anti–Vietnam War movement in America, had grown mistrustful of the establishment and sought to defy its codes of behavior. Author Margaret O. Hyde notes that the reality of heroin abuse forced itself into the American psyche:

> [Heroin abuse] moved out of the slums and ghettos to infect the sons and daughters of well-to-do citizens of middle-class America. The alarm sounded across the country at that time did not emanate from concern about the long-standing drug abuse problems in racial ghettos, but rather was a result of "dope" reaching white youths in "good" neighborhoods. Patterns of narcotic use dominant in the well-known drug communities . . . "rippled out" to other communities: Palo Alto, California; Ann Arbor, Michigan; Phoenix, Arizona; Grenell, Ohio; and Bar Harbor, Maine, are just a few. . . . Shocked, distraught, unbelieving parents who discovered that their son or daughter was a heroin addict demanded government and community response to deal with the crisis. Investigations revealed that young, teen-age white boys and girls, just like the boys and girls in the slums, rob, steal, and prostitute themselves, or "hustle," on the streets to support drug habits of $25, $50, and even $150 a day. [12]

Heroin also became an increasing concern of the U.S. military throughout the Vietnam War as American military personnel stationed in Southeast Asia encountered heroin that was inexpensive, pure, and readily available from the nearby "Golden Triangle." Military officials eventually estimated that one out of every five U.S. soldiers had become addicted to the drug during their tour of duty in Vietnam.

At the end of the 1960s, President Richard M. Nixon declared a war on drugs, urging Congress to pass a bill for $370 million to fight the heroin epidemic.

By the decade's end, law enforcement and health officials estimated the number of heroin users in the United States to be in excess of 1 million. In response to this startling statistic, President Richard M. Nixon declared a war on drugs in a statement to Congress, and urged them to pass a $370 million appropriations bill to fight the heroin epidemic. The bill led to the implementation of federal programs to educate the public, expand treatment opportunities, and strengthen drug traffic control. Additionally, the military's new Special Action Office for Drug Abuse Prevention instituted mandatory drug testing and required returning Vietnam War veterans who tested positive for the drug to undergo treatment. In 1973 the number of heroin users finally began to subside and would be fewer than four hundred thousand by the decade's end. Hyde attributes this decline in use to "changing public attitude and increased financial support for education, research, and treatment, as well as a more balanced law enforcement approach toward the control of the distribution and supply of heroin."[13]

As heroin use diminished during the 1970s, however, cocaine use caught on with the American middle and upper classes, and its widespread popularity would eventually help widespread heroin use to reemerge. Cocaine use became increasingly accepted in society as a sign of social status and affluence during the 1970s, and media coverage of the drug's use among the rich and famous enhanced its glamorous image and legitimized its use in society. "For many Americans," explains Hyde, "cocaine became the symbol of fast-track living which lasted well into the 1980's. . . . In this period of liberalization, only the social consensus against heroin held firm, largely because . . . its use had long been associated with criminals and social outcasts."[14] With its estimated 2.2 million users by the late 1980s, however, cocaine use also escalated to epidemic levels. Connotations of status began to fade as cocaine addiction wrought increasing havoc in the lives of users across the American socioeconomic spectrum—but particularly among crack cocaine users in the inner city. By the early 1990s, cocaine lost its

---

Baltimore: The Heroin Capital of the United States

Though Baltimore already had an abnormally high degree of heroin abuse before the U.S. heroin epidemic of the 1990s, the city came to be widely considered by health and law enforcement officials as the heroin capital of the nation at the beginning of the twenty-first century. When Baltimore became a key East Coast distribution point for high-purity South American heroin during the mid-1990s, its street heroin became more pure, and thus more addictive and more deadly, than that of most other cities in the nation, and its heroin use rate began to skyrocket.

In the year 2000 alone, there were more than three hundred fatal heroin-related overdoses in Baltimore and a similar number of heroin-related hospital emergencies. With official estimates of one out of every ten Baltimore residents addicted to heroin by 2001—some sixty thousand men and women, the majority of whom were believed to use the drug intravenously—the problem became so serious that the federal government designated the city a "high intensity drug trafficking area," making it eligible for special federal assistance to local police.

standing as the nation's drug of choice, and the number of users significantly declined.

Cocaine Cartels Enter the Heroin Trade

With cocaine sales rapidly diminishing in the United States during the early 1990s, drug cartels in Colombia who had supplied the lucrative cocaine market for nearly two decades began to diversify from cocaine to the higher-profit, more easily manufactured heroin. They hired experts from Southeast Asia to teach them opium-cultivating and heroin-processing techniques, and expansive poppy fields began to appear along the eastern slopes of the Central Andean Mountain ranges in central Colombia. Just as cocaine had been, raw opium was transported from the fields, often through hidden jungle trails but also through sea and air routes, to concealed laboratories that were far from the opium-growing regions of the country.

Though new to opium growing and heroin manufacturing, the drug cartels needed no lessons in the secrets of drug trafficking. Their location close to the United States had always been extremely strategic for smuggling. Colombia's coastlines on both the Pacific Ocean and the Caribbean Sea provided smugglers a near-infinite variety of air, land, and sea drug-smuggling routes.

Heroin, like cocaine, was smuggled over the U.S. border in many ways. Couriers swallowed small quantities of heroin in balloons or hid the drug inside hollowed-out shoes, luggage, and clothing. Large shipments of the drug were concealed within manufactured goods that were imported into the United States from Latin America.

To compete in the U.S. heroin market, which had long been dominated by Southeast Asian heroin, these Colombian cartels did what had proven so effective for the Mafia earlier in the century: they undercut the competition with inexpensive, high-purity heroin. The entrance of these new suppliers into the American heroin market had dramatic repercussions—not only in the United States but also on the entire global heroin market. When Southeast Asian heroin began to match the purity level and price of Colombian heroin, an ongoing price and purity war resulted. As more and more people around the

Drug cartels in Colombia began manufacturing and trafficking heroin in the 1990s. Pictured is a Colombian heroin confiscation.

world began to experiment with this super-potent and inexpensive heroin, a global heroin epidemic began. By 1995 there were an estimated 10 million heroin users worldwide, with large numbers of users in Canada, Great Britain, and the United States, as well as in Europe, the former Soviet Union, and Asia.

The Global Heroin Epidemic's Impact on the United States

In the United States, this competition between heroin suppliers brought unprecedented levels of heroin purity. "During the [1980s]," states the Drug Enforcement Administration, "the purity of street heroin ranged from one to ten percent; more recently, the purity of heroin, especially that from South America, has skyrocketed to rates as high as 98 percent."[15] This newfound purity brought significant changes in the way the drug was used. In the past, when heroin had been of low strength, its use was limited to those who were willing to inject the drug to obtain a strong high. With this dramatic increase in the purity of heroin during the 1990s, however, it became possible for beginning users to use noninjection methods to obtain an extremely strong dosage of the drug. One method that gained popularity was the snorting of "lines" of heroin in the same manner that cocaine was used. Another popular method was heroin smoking, often referred to by users as "chasing the dragon" because of the curly, dragonlike wisps of smoke that rise from burning heroin.

This ability to use heroin through noninjection methods made the drug far more attractive and less frightening to many Americans. Heroin came to have connotations of style and glamour with increasing numbers of middle- and upper-class adults, just as cocaine

Common paraphernalia for heroin use includes hypodermic needles and spoons.

had in the 1970s and 1980s. Though heroin was still available on the streets of the inner city in twenty-five to fifty-dollar bags, spoons, or balloons, under nicknames such as H, horse, boy, skag, and smack, it was now also sold in chic nightclubs and suburban living rooms. A 320 percent usage increase between 1992 and 1994 alone created an unprecedented heroin epidemic in the United States, with entirely new demographics of users.

The drug's new popularity among adults was matched by increased heroin use among the nation's teens, as evidenced by the nearly quadrupled number of heroin-related emergency room episodes among youths aged twelve to seventeen between 1991 and 1995. Widespread addiction resulted among many of these ill-informed young users. Dr. Alan Leshner, director of the National Institute on Drug Abuse (NIDA), notes, "Many young people have a naive belief that because they are snorting or smoking heroin and not injecting it, their heroin use is not addictive. This is a dangerous misconception." [16]

Throughout the 1990s, a growing number of young heroin users found that they had grossly misjudged the drug's addictiveness, and that their once-casual use had quickly become a daily habit. In 2000, statistics confirmed what health officials had feared about the widespread experimentation with heroin among teens: increasing numbers of them were turning to injection as a more efficient means of using the drug. Further, many adult users who had previously avoided the drug because of the social stigmas attached to the use of

Heroin Snorting on the Rise

According to a survey conducted by the Substance Abuse and Mental Health Services Administration (SAMHSA), a significant increase in the number of Americans experimenting with heroin snorting accompanied the rise in the purity of street heroin in the United States during the early 1990s. The survey, which was conducted between 1988 and 1993, revealed that the annual number of hospital emergency department visits related to snorting or sniffing heroin jumped by 470 percent, from eleven hundred to six thousand. However, the hospital emergencies related to snorting composed just 20 percent of the total increase in heroin-related emergencies over this period.

needles now found that they, too, had insatiable intravenous heroin habits—because their fear of injecting the drug had been surpassed by their fear of the drug's painful withdrawal symptoms.

The Epidemic Continues

By the late 1990s, the heroin marketplace in the United States shifted yet again as drug cartels in Mexico began to eclipse Southeast Asian heroin suppliers as the main competition of Colombian heroin cartels. Mexican drug syndicates quickly seized a rapidly growing share of the U.S. heroin business, and by the decade's end had come to dominate the heroin market west of the Mississippi River. As a result of these new entrants into the U.S. heroin arena, the price and purity wars that had spawned the epidemic during the early 1990s were still present as the decade drew to a close.

Though the alarming growth rate of the epidemic had slowed and even reversed in some regions of the United States by the year 2000, it had increased in others—particularly in the northeastern seaboard, where much of the nation's Colombian heroin was smuggled into the country—leaving experts divided on the question of whether the heroin epidemic in America had finally begun to subside. While the NIDA believed that the nation's overall use of heroin in America was in decline, other estimates suggested that the epidemic had yet to reach its peak. In either event, with an estimated 1.5 million heroin users from across America's socioeconomic spectrum at the dawn of the twenty-first century, 980,000 of whom are believed to be hard-core addicts, it is once again clear that the drug holds allure to people from all socioeconomic standings, races, and ages.

Chapter 3

Consequences of Heroin Addiction

Though the price of street heroin in the United States has never been lower, the ultimate costs of heroin addiction remain extremely high. With heroin addiction comes a wide range of consequences, not only for addicts themselves but also for their friends and families, as well as for the societies in which they live.

The Health Consequences for Addicts

The health consequences for heroin addicts are numerous, and many of them are extremely serious. The most serious threat of all is the ever-present possibility of taking a fatal overdose of the drug. When heroin overdose occurs, the drug's depressant effect on the respiratory system prevents the body from getting a sufficient amount of oxygen, and the user falls into a coma. The user's respiratory system continues to slow to the point where the body simply loses its impulse to breathe. As no oxygen whatsoever reaches the bloodstream, the user goes into cardiac arrest and dies. With the purity level of street heroin currently ranging from zero to 90 percent, it is extremely easy for users to underestimate the strength of a new batch of the drug and overdose on it.

The purity level of a given batch of heroin is dictated by how much "cut" (additive) has been mixed with the drug by dealers who seek to increase their sales profits. Since users have no way of knowing what substances have been added to heroin, additional danger lies in the possibility that poisonous agents are present in the drug. Common heroin additives include relatively harmless substances such as sugar, powdered milk, quinine, and cocoa; however, varying amounts of highly toxic substances such as powdered soap and kitchen cleanser frequently appear in street heroin as well, and can cause death by poisoning. "Heroin," notes the Do It Now Foundation, "is the end product in an intricate chain of manufacture that spans continents and involves dozens of separate operations and uncounted greedy middlemen."[17] Thus, it is virtually impossible to tell how pure street heroin is, or, for that matter, whether the substance contains any heroin at all, simply by looking at it.

This heroin user never revived after falling into a coma. Heroin depresses the body's respiratory system, often resulting in unconsciousness.

Additional risk of overdose lies in the inadvertent purchase of synthetic substances that are passed off as heroin. This so-called designer heroin contains no actual heroin whatsoever, but is in reality either fentanyl or meperidine—both synthetic drugs made in makeshift laboratories. Though indistinguishable from heroin in appearance and taste, fentanyl can be hundreds or even thousands of times stronger than pure heroin. The National Institute on Drug Abuse cautions that some fentanyl purchased on the street is so lethal in strength, "users have been found dead with the needle used to inject the drug still in their arms."[18] In some instances, meperidine has caused brain damage and ultimately paralysis in users.

Physical Addiction

The main concern of heroin addicts, however, isn't to avoid lethal overdose or poisoning. Rather it is to avoid the most obvious and immediate health consequence of addiction: the sickening "withdrawal" symptoms that begin anew every time a heroin dose wears off. Depending on how severe the physical addiction is, a heroin addict in withdrawal will experience flulike symptoms that, among others, include sneezing, running nose and eyes, alternate bouts of profuse sweating and cold flashes, muscle and bone pain, abdominal cramps, diarrhea, vomiting, and muscle spasms. Heroin addicts therefore crave heroin not only to feel its pleasure, but also to avoid the pain and sickness that come with not getting a fix every few hours. This all-consuming nature of heroin addiction is summed up by poet and longtime heroin addict William S. Burroughs: "Junk [heroin] is not . . . a means to increased enjoyment of life. Junk is not a kick. It is a way of life."[19]

A person begins to experience withdrawal-related physical symptoms after a few weeks of steady heroin use. Though medical science has long known that heroin addiction and its withdrawal symptoms involve the central nervous system in some way, brain researchers from Johns Hopkins University made a remarkable discovery in 1972 that lent tremendous insight into the nature of physical addiction to heroin and withdrawal from the drug.

Poet William S. Burroughs described his heroin use as "a way of life."

These researchers found that the human brain's nerve cells, known as neurons, have receptor sites that seem specifically designed to feel the effects of heroin and other opiate drugs. They found that opium molecules fit into these receptors like a key fits into a lock, and cause the nervous system to relieve pain and create feelings of euphoria. This was a puzzling discovery for these researchers, since it seemed extremely unlikely that nature would provide the human brain with receptors designed for the molecules of a specific type of plant. They suspected that there must be another purpose for these receptor sites.

Endorphin Research

Researchers later discovered that the body naturally manufactures chemicals called endorphins to maintain a general sense of well-being in humans and to regulate certain bodily functions. When the body experiences pain or stress, it releases large quantities of endorphins to kill pain. Additional research revealed that opium and

Chemical Structure of Heroin

$$R = R_1 = H, \text{Morphine}$$
$$R = R_1 = COCH_3, \text{Heroin}$$
$$R = CH_3, R_1 = H, \text{Codine}$$

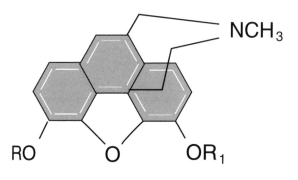

human endorphins are identical to one another in their molecular makeup and, therefore, in their effects on the body. Thus, not only is heroin able to perfectly mimic the effects of endorphins, but since the drug's molecules are usually present in far greater quantities than those of naturally occurring endorphins, its effects on the body are considerably stronger.

Endorphin researchers have also found that as a user's body attempts to adapt to the near-constant presence of heroin, significant chemical and physical changes take place in the brain. The brain senses an overabundance of what it thinks are endorphins, and attempts to restore balance to itself by shutting down its own production of real endorphins. It continues to do so whether or not the addict is currently high on heroin. The addict's body must therefore depend entirely on heroin to regulate the various bodily functions that are no longer regulated by endorphins. When there is no heroin present, these functions cease to operate properly, thereby triggering the wide variety of symptoms associated with withdrawal.

Another way that the heroin addict's body attempts to restore balance to itself is by making its various systems, including the nervous system, resistant to the effects of heroin. This resistance to the drug's effects, known as "tolerance," steadily increases for as long as the addict continues to use the drug without interruption. As an addict's tolerance increases, so does the amount of heroin needed to produce the drug's original effects. The severity of withdrawal symptoms likewise increases. Tolerance to heroin increases extremely quickly and causes the need for dosages that would easily cause lethal overdose in first-time users. For example, while first-time users may need as little as two to five milligrams to get high, long-term addicts typically need hundreds of milligrams a day just to take the edge off their withdrawal symptoms. (An addict never grows immune to overdose, however—some amount of heroin will always prove fatal.)

Once addiction has progressed to a relatively high point of tolerance, most addicts switch to intravenous heroin injection to get the strongest possible dosage, and this form of drug use exposes them to an enormous array of illnesses. "To know . . . an injecting drug user as a patient," explains Dr. Gabor D. Kelen of Johns Hopkins University School of Medicine, "is to know medicine, because they pretty well get just about every possible medical condition known to man." [20]

The Consequences of Long-Term Heroin Use

The Drug Abuse Research Center at the University of California at Los Angeles began a study in 1964 in which 581 male heroin addicts in their early twenties were monitored over the course of thirty years in an effort to determine the survival rate and long-term physical effects of heroin addiction. The results of the study, published on Doctor's Guide Online, were alarming. After thirty years, the study showed that 284 of the original 581 participants—more than half—had died. Of these deceased participants, 22 percent died of overdose, 15 percent died of chronic liver disease, and 20 percent died from homicide or suicide. Many of the remaining 43 percent died of either cancer, cardiovascular diseases, or AIDS. Of the 297 participants who were still alive after thirty years, 43 percent were still using heroin.

Sharing Hypodermic Needles

One reason that heroin addicts suffer from so many illnesses is that they, like other intravenous drug addicts, share hypodermic needles, thereby spreading infectious diseases. Shared needles transmit disease so easily that an estimated 90 percent of all intravenous drug users in the United States have some type of infectious disease. In 1996 the Centers for Disease Control and Prevention declared that the sharing of drug needles accounted for "about one-third of all new cases of AIDS in the U.S. each year."[21] A high percentage of addicts who develop AIDS also contract tuberculosis, an infectious disease that can attack lung tissue, lymph glands, or other parts of the body.

Other potentially fatal diseases widely transmitted by the sharing of needles include the hepatitis B virus (HBV) and the hepatitis C virus (HCV), both of which cause serious damage to the liver. "Of those addicts who . . . inject their drugs intravenously with a needle," explains James W. West of the Betty Ford Center, a treatment facility for drug addiction founded by the former First Lady,

Former First Lady Betty Ford founded the Betty Ford Center for Substance Abuse Rehabilitation.

Chronic Constipation

A particularly unpleasant health condition that virtually all heroin addicts suffer is chronic constipation. Though opium provides relief for an upset stomach, heroin intensifies opium's soothing properties to the point of impairing the efficiency and function of the small intestines, resulting in chronic constipation for heroin addicts. This backup in the small intestines causes severe pain and tenderness in the addict's lower abdomen and colon, and can also cause related physical discomforts such as headache and backache. Additionally, since the bacteria and toxins that should be eliminated remain instead in the lower intestines for a prolonged period of time, some of them are reabsorbed back into the body, which further weakens the immune system and places the organs, particularly the liver, under additional stress. Further, the addict's body does not develop tolerance to this effect of heroin—it is a constant for as long as the physical addiction exists.

about 80 percent have hepatitis B and at least 50 percent also contract hepatitis C. There is a virtual epidemic of this viral liver infection among IV drug users. . . . Some who become infected progress to full-blown chronic active hepatitis with eventual cirrhosis, while others develop a chronic carrier state that makes one prone to cancer of the liver. Most, however, will recover from the condition if they stop re-infecting themselves with dirty needles.[22]

Additionally, all sexually transmitted diseases, including gonorrhea, syphilis, and herpes, can be contracted through the sharing of needles. The high incidence of prostitution among the addict community contributes even further to this high infection rate among intravenous drug users.

The range of infections that intravenous drug users commonly suffer is not limited to those that can be contracted by sharing infected needles, however. "The very act of injecting foreign substances, in particular heroin," notes Dr. Kelen, "depresses the immunity of the patient or user and so they are open to infections."[23] Among those noncontagious infections that intravenous drug users widely experience are skin infections at the site of injection, which can result in skin ulcers, abscesses, fungal infections, botulism, tetanus, stroke, destruction of lung tissue, and infection of the heart valves and linings. Additionally, long-term intravenous drug use often results in collapsed veins, arthritis, and other related illnesses.

Compounding these and all other heroin-related physical illnesses are the poor dietary and sleeping habits that addicts generally practice. Further, the ailments that heroin addicts suffer tend to go untreated, because the drug's pain-relieving properties conceal symptoms of real physical illness. Even when addicts are aware of their ailments, they are often afraid to seek medical help for fear of forced withdrawal and incarceration.

Psychological Addiction to Heroin

Addiction to heroin sets in motion very damaging and complex psychological consequences for the addict, in addition to its harmful physiological consequences. Like many other drug addictions, heroin addiction halts the emotional development of users at whatever developmental stage their addiction began, and diminishes existing emotional coping skills. Since emotional discomfort, as well as physical pain, is relieved by heroin use, the drug can initially make experiences that might otherwise be unpleasant more enjoyable. However, the more often heroin is used for this purpose, the less able the user is to cope with such situations without the drug. One recovering heroin addict states:

> [The addict] finds that certain events are not merely better on the drug but cannot be faced without it: a visit to the bank manager, a job interview, a meal with his parents. Each time he surrenders to the temptation, this feeling increases so that the next time it is harder to resist. Even his increasingly brief glimpses of the trap into which he is walking serve, perversely, not to strengthen his resolve but to weaken it: he wants the escapism of heroin to forget what he is doing. [24]

Additional evidence of psychological addiction lies in the overwhelming depression that accompanies the physical discomfort of withdrawal, as well as in the acute anxiety that stems from the knowledge that heroin, the cure for the sickness, is available, if only some way can be found to obtain it. Obtaining the drug becomes the overriding ambition of the addict's life, and no amount of effort toward this end seems irrational or excessive. Steven Tyler, lead singer of the rock band Aerosmith, recalls the days before he and his bandmates went into recovery for heroin addiction: "We used to spend all day to cop [obtain the drug] and if we got it by the end of

Lead singer Steven Tyler, and other members of the rock band Aerosmith, have undergone treatment for heroin addiction.

the night, we were happy. All of the energy we put out all day long and all of the misery and lies, all of the grief that we put up with to cop those drugs was an insane, intense vim and vigor."[25]

Antisocial Behavior

As psychological addiction progresses, heroin users find themselves less and less interested in friends and family members who do not share their obsession, and they begin to seek the company of those who do. The relationships between hard-core addicts cannot accurately be described as friendships, however, since they lack the trust and the empathy that characterizes friendship, and are instead more akin to impersonal alliances formed in pursuit of a shared, daily goal. Recovering heroin addict Anthony Kiedis, lead singer of the Red Hot Chili Peppers, notes the antisocial aspect of heroin addiction: "Without you realizing what's happening, heroin sucks the love out of you. . . . It's very deceiving because it'll numb a pain, but it'll numb your love as well."[26]

One Addict's Regrets

In the following passage from Jara A. Krivanek's book, *Heroin: Myths and Reality,* a former heroin addict tells of some of the consequences of her addiction:

I'm 29 years old. I wish that, by now, my career was all settled for me. That I had friends. You don't learn how to be a friend or what a relationship is when you're just getting high. And when you stop getting high, it's like being a baby and starting all over again from the beginning. When you're high, it's like being a robot. It's euphoric, but you could be anybody. All the people that are out there using drugs, the faces change, but they're all the same, they're all nobodies, because they're never going anywhere, they're never going to make anything of themselves. . . .

The main thing that bothers me is that the years that I lost while I was taking dope I will never get back. And you lose a lot of self-pride because of the things you end up doing, and it takes a long time to get that back. What I should have been doing all that time in my life was going to college, pursuing a career, and going out and doing the so-called normal things. What I was doing was hanging out on the street corner and getting high. And that was my whole life. You don't see a lot of things when you get high. . . . If I hadn't gotten involved with drugs, maybe I would have had a career. Maybe I would have had more confidence in myself at this point in my life, because I don't have it now. I'd have some friends today, which I don't have now because after all those years, I really didn't have any friends left.

Heroin can emotionally desensitize its addicts to the point where many addicts will commit crimes to obtain money necessary for the drug. For the desperate addict, offenses that would have seemed unconscionable before addiction occurred—crimes such as burglary, armed robbery, assault, in some cases even murder—no longer seem abhorrent. As the downward spiral of addiction continues, it becomes increasingly difficult for addicts to face themselves or their actions, and thus, to imagine themselves ever reentering mainstream society.

Particularly grim evidence of the extent to which heroin addicts can be in denial of the consequences of their actions lies in the many addicted mothers who continue to use the drug during pregnancy. The pregnancies of many heroin-addicted women end in spontaneous abortions triggered by withdrawal symptoms. Full-term babies who are born to these women are as physically addicted to the drug as their mothers, and will begin to experience withdrawal symptoms shortly after birth. Because these infants have no psychological dependence, they are particularly receptive to addiction-curing medical treatment if their addiction is diagnosed. Left untreated, however, the addiction can result in the infant's death. Further, even successfully treated heroin-addicted babies are at greater risk of sudden infant death syndrome (SIDS), and many of them have contracted the HIV virus from their mothers.

Despite a heroin addict's best efforts to maintain emotional oblivion through heroin intoxication, however, feelings of guilt and loss of dignity, as well as an acute awareness of the self-imposed alienation from family, friends, and society, cannot be entirely avoided. "I remember sitting at a table," recalls one recovering addict of the sense of helplessness he felt from his addiction, "in front of me an open packet of heroin, containing, I reckoned, enough to kill myself. I tried to think of a single reason not to do so. I couldn't." [27]

A well-publicized example of someone whose heroin addiction did ultimately lead to suicide is the rock star Kurt Cobain of the band Nirvana. Cobain, an intravenous heroin addict, killed himself with a shotgun on April 5, 1994. (Coroners also determined, however, that his

Intravenous heroin addict Kurt Cobain, from the rock band Nirvana, committed suicide by shooting himself with a gun immediately after injecting himself with a lethal dose of heroin.

body contained three times the lethal level of heroin at the time of his death, and that he would soon have died of overdose if he hadn't shot himself.) Cobain had threatened to commit suicide repeatedly in the weeks before his death, and had also overdosed several times during this period but had been revived with emergency medical treatment. In the suicide note that he left his wife, rock star Courtney Love, Cobain stated that their two-year-old daughter, Francis Bean Cobain, would lead a much happier life without him. As with Kurt Cobain, many addicts succumb to their desperation and commit suicide.

The Consequences for Others

Cobain's suicide provides an extreme example of the extent to which the consequences of heroin addiction can extend beyond addicts themselves to include their families and friends. The consequences of heroin addiction are not limited to the relatives of addicts who have died, however, but also affect those who have addicted loved ones who are still living. In addition to feeling powerless to do

The consequences of heroin addiction can be enormous financially, physically, and emotionally. Pictured are heroin addicts in a detoxification clinic.

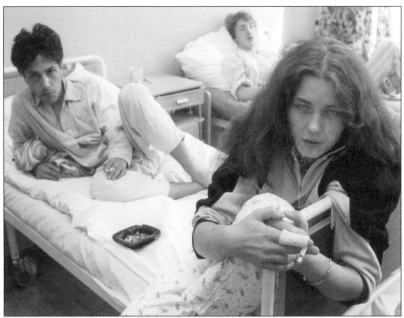

anything but watch their loved ones inflict ongoing physical and psychological suffering on themselves, for example, they must also contend with the daily fear that the addict might either succumb to despair and commit suicide or die from lethal overdose. Moreover, since many hard-core heroin addicts in withdrawal steal from anyone, including family, to obtain money with which to purchase the drug, relatives often suffer from painful feelings of betrayal.

Society, too, must pay a high price for the heroin addiction in its midst. Law enforcement efforts to control the many illegal activities associated with the heroin trade are extremely costly, as is the incarceration of those convicted of these activities. And, as is true of most illegal drugs in America, heroin dealing increases the amount of street violence. Dr. Kelen explains that next to overdose,

> the second or . . . possibly even an equally . . . common cause for [heroin related] death indirectly is shootings. . . . Many of the shootings are related to local disagreements with [drug dealers] and so unfortunately, the ugly side of that reality is the patients come in shot and dead, and not only the drug users or those involved in the trade. We often see very innocent bystanders, including young children, who just happen to get in the way.[28]

The practice of intravenous heroin use takes an additional toll on society by spreading infectious diseases, as well as by putting the health care workers who provide care to addicts at considerable risk of contracting these illnesses. Further, the combined expenses to the federal, state, and local levels of government for the health care and social services provided to heroin addicts are enormous. In 1995 alone, for example, the cost to the nation for the estimated seventy-six thousand heroin-related emergency room episodes is estimated to be well in excess of $200 million. This figure does not include the cost of publicly funded detox centers and rehabilitation clinics, nor the many other services provided to homeless and destitute hard-core addicts.

The price paid for heroin addiction—in loss of life, suffering, and financial expense—is high indeed for all concerned. The wide range of consequences that accompany heroin addiction points to the tremendous need for effective and practical measures to prevent experimentation with the drug to the greatest extent possible.

 **Chapter 4**

Preventing
Heroin Abuse

Twentieth-century events clearly demonstrated that simply making heroin illegal was not enough to eliminate the demand for the drug in the United States. Nor have the best efforts of the nation's legislators, law enforcement officials, and diplomats abroad been enough to keep resourceful heroin traffickers from supplying this demand. Thus, a method of effectively eliminating the demand for the drug has long been sought by public health officials and medical experts. Finding such a method, however, has been exceedingly difficult because the causes of heroin abuse have proven to be numerous and complex.

Differing Opinions on Heroin Prevention

Opinions differ in the United States on what causes the problem of drug abuse in general, and heroin abuse in particular, and these opinions have resulted in a variety of approaches to prevention. "The approaches based on these opinions have developed through recent decades," explains the directors of the Haight Ashbury Free Clinic in San Francisco, "[with] one or another gaining ascendancy, depending often on the prevailing attitudes about drugs, politics, young people and a number of other factors." [29] As additional abuse prevention approaches emerge, experts grow even more divided over how the nation's limited allocation of prevention funds should be spent.

Experts do widely agree on a few basic premises of heroin prevention. One is the belief that heroin-abuse prevention is an extremely high-stakes endeavor, and that its primary objective should be to guard vulnerable children and teens from the drug's dangers. Another widely accepted premise is summed up by Barry McCaffrey, director of the Office of National Drug Control Policy: "Since most drug users do not begin with heroin, but turn to heroin after using other drugs, the most useful heroin prevention efforts are those aimed at keeping young people away from [those other] drugs in the first place."[30] Consequently, the prevention of heroin abuse and the prevention of the abuse of these so-called gateway drugs are often considered synonymous by prevention experts.

Yet another premise that is commonly embraced by experts holds that an ill-conceived drug abuse prevention strategy can be more than just ineffective; it can backfire and result in increased experimentation with a given drug. The potential for such a pitfall was

U.S. drug czar Barry McCaffrey believes that prevention of heroin abuse should begin by warning youth about the dangers of less harmful drugs, called gateway drugs.

demonstrated by the first drug abuse prevention effort in the United States. Launched during the 1930s, this strategy did feature some understanding of the link between the use of gateway drugs such as marijuana and eventual experimentation with potentially lethal drugs such as heroin. This approach featured little understanding of human nature, however, and sought to keep young people away from all drugs by using scare tactics, exaggerations, and falsehoods about marijuana. *Reefer Madness,* an educational film made by the Federal Bureau of Narcotics during the late 1930s, was the epitome of this prevention approach. "The film depicts the downfall of a promising young man after one puff of marijuana," author Mathea Falcon writes: "Instantly he becomes violent, abusive, and sexually aggressive, shocking his friends and his boss, and ending his chances

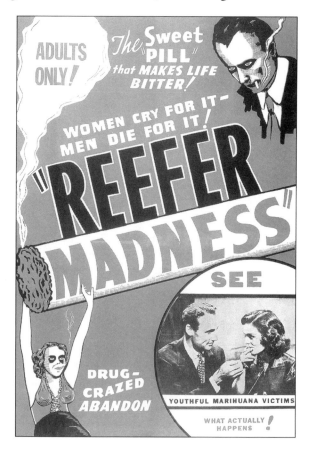

Intended to educate young people about the dangers of drugs, the film Reefer Madness *relied on scare tactics and exaggerations rather than facts.*

for success. The message is clear: Marijuana has transformed a son of the middle class into a crazed criminal." [31]

Since, as was the case with illegal heroin use, illegal marijuana use prior to the 1960s occurred for the most part in lower-class, inner-city areas, and out of the view of the majority of Americans, this image of the lunatic marijuana user prevailed in the United States for many years. During the early 1960s, however, the growing number of young people who were opposed to American involvement in the Vietnam War began to mistrust and question many of the standards and values long held by society. Among the many things they began to reevaluate was what they had been told about marijuana, and use of the drug began to trickle into the middle class.

As more and more teens discovered that the drug had been misrepresented, the damages of the scare tactics that had been employed for decades were twofold: not only was the legitimate harmfulness of marijuana use overshadowed by the absurd exaggerations, but the serious dangers that had been attributed to drugs such as heroin were dismissed by teens as more lies. Epidemics of both marijuana and heroin abuse occurred among teens during the 1960s, and the film *Reefer Madness* became a cult favorite among drug-using young people throughout the United States.

Straight Talk

Faced with a complete loss of credibility by the late 1960s for having employed what had come to be known as the *Reefer Madness* approach to prevention, educators and public health officials sought to identify the cause of drug abuse. Many arrived at the conclusion that the central cause was lack of accurate information about various drugs. Based on the belief that an appeal to reason would be an effective drug abuse deterrent for young people, a fact-based drug prevention approach emerged, and it remains a component of most approaches that have emerged in subsequent years. Often called "straight talk," this approach focuses on providing accurate, detailed information about the psychoactive effects and specific consequences of commonly abused drugs.

As part of a $370 million appropriations bill passed by Congress to fight the heroin epidemic, the Drug Abuse Education Act of

"Life Enhancement"

In the following passage from their book, *DrugFree: A Unique, Positive Approach to Staying Off Alcohol and Other Drugs,* Richard Seymour and David E. Smith, M.D., argue that very concept of drug-abuse prevention places too much importance on the practice of abusing drugs:

> There is a passage in the [ancient Chinese spiritual text] *I Ching* that says you cannot fight the devil directly. When you do, you tend to become the devil that you are fighting. Instead, the Chinese oracle recommends that you fight the devil by emphasizing what is good and allowing that to replace the darkness. In that sense, we dislike the very phrase "prevention." We dislike it because the core of what needs to be done is misrepresented by the term. Prevention sounds like a limiting, the creating of taboos in order to circumscribe behavior. What is needed by young people—by everyone, for that matter—is not limiting but expanding, not curtailing freedom but increasing it by providing opportunities for growth and development that make the use of drugs superfluous.
>
> We feel that a better term than prevention is "life enhancement," a process whereby people work together for mutual growth. People are ideally called upon to help themselves and one another by developing their own potential to the highest degree, practicing the principles they have learned in all their affairs and carrying their own physical and spiritual awakening to others.

1970 provided substantial funding for the rapid implementation of the straight-talk prevention approach in public schools and other public forums throughout the nation. Statistics showed that heroin use did significantly decline during the years following the implementation of the straight-talk approach. Based on these encouraging initial results, straight talk remained the nation's chief prevention approach for over a decade.

Not all researchers believed that misinformation had been the primary reason for the epidemic of heroin and other drug abuse during the 1960s, nor did they believe that providing detailed information about drugs would be enough to prevent another such epidemic in the future. People also questioned the extent to which straight talk was responsible for declining heroin use during the 1970s—particularly since the approach was implemented at a time when the number of heroin treatment programs in the United States increased and the government began to crack down on heroin-manufacturing nations in Southeast Asia. The correlation between straight talk and the reduction in heroin use was questioned further with the simultaneous and substantial rise in the number of cocaine users in the United States during the 1970s.

Despite the straight-talk approach being vigorously administered throughout the nation for a decade, the use of cocaine was rapidly approaching epidemic levels by the beginning of the 1980s. Since this rise in cocaine use seemed to be inspired in large part by the glamorous and worldly connotations that the drug now held for many in society, some researchers began to suspect that the main cause of drug abuse was social pressure to use drugs, rather than lack of accurate information about them. From this theory, the "resistance-training" approach to prevention emerged, and remains the predominant prevention approach in the United States for heroin and other drugs to the present day.

Resistance Training

The first resistance-training research program, Project S.M.A.R.T. (Self-Management and Resistance Training), was launched in 1981 by the University of Southern California. Experiments with this new prevention approach did feature some degree of straight talk about heroin and other drugs, but its main emphasis was on finding ways for young people to resist the social influences and pressures that were suspected to be the cause of drug experimentation.

Project S.M.A.R.T.'s founders suspected that, as with so many patterns of human behavior, people's susceptibility to peer pressure is largely determined before they reach their teens, and that it is therefore imperative to provide resistance skills at this stage of children's development—before social pressure to try drugs begins. The two main ways that they hoped resistance training would prevent drug abuse was to first provide young people with the self-esteem needed to resist the pressure to use drugs, and then to provide them with specific methods for refusing drugs. Clinical trials of Project S.M.A.R.T. conducted in the Los Angeles Unified School District suggested that children at the fifth-grade level were the most receptive to learning resistance skills, and that resistance training did hold significant promise for preventing these children from experimenting with gateway drugs.

Based on Project S.M.A.R.T.'s promising research results, a number of resistance-training prevention campaigns were developed during the early 1980s, and two were particularly well funded and implemented nationwide. The first of these was then First Lady Nancy Reagan's massive "Just Say No" campaign. Launched in 1981, "Just Say No" employed a variety of methods of raising self-esteem, and provided simple phrases (thus, the name "Just Say No") for young people to employ when pressured to use drugs. Reagan promoted "Just Say No" throughout the United States and around the world over the course of the following eight years.

As part of her "Just Say No" campaign, former First Lady Nancy Reagan appeared on the Good Morning America *show on October 12, 1983.*

The second of these two large-scale resistance-training campaigns began two years after the creation of "Just Say No." Called Project Drug Abuse Resistance Education (Project D.A.R.E.), this was a joint effort between Los Angeles police chief Darrel Gates and Project S.M.A.R.T.'s original developers. Project D.A.R.E.'s curriculum was quite similar to that of "Just Say No" and numerous other resistance-training campaigns that were emerging at that time, with one major exception: it was taught in fifth- or sixth-grade classrooms by uniformed police officers, rather than by classroom teachers. Project D.A.R.E. quickly surpassed the Just Say No campaign as the national standard in drug abuse prevention during the 1980s, and by the 1990s police departments were presenting it in 75 percent of the nation's school districts.

Social Pressure to Use Heroin

For advocates of D.A.R.E. and other lesser-known resistance-training programs, the heroin epidemic that began during the 1990s is a worst-case scenario of young people under pressure to use drugs. Many young people—and even adults—first experimented with heroin under the assumption that noninjection methods of use are nonaddictive and safe. However, at least as many began using it with some awareness of its danger, and this very danger is what led them to try it.

Resistance-training advocates suggest that among some young people, social status is to be gained by risking heroin's danger. Large-scale dealers often give dangerous-sounding names to their heroin to assure its notoriety, and to instill customer recognition and loyalty. Among the more popular brands of street heroin are "No Way Out," "Death Wish," "Body Bag," "Poison," "Dead on Arrival," and "Next Stop Heaven."

The widespread appeal of heroin's danger is also reflected in the startling reaction of many young people to the heroin-overdose death in 1996 of keyboardist Jonathan Melvoin of the rock band The Smashing Pumpkins. Though one might have expected Melvoin's overdose death to have discouraged the use of heroin at least somewhat, the opposite seems to have occurred. Immediately following his death, there was a dramatic increase in the demand for

Janis Joplin is one of many celebrities who have died of a heroin overdose. Resistance-training advocates suggest that heroin's popularity among celebrities is a cause of heroin experimentation among young people.

"Red Rum" heroin—the dangerously potent brand on which he overdosed ("Red Rum" is "murder" spelled backward).

For resistance-training advocates, this irrational response to the tragic death of a celebrity also gives profound insight into the origins of the social pressure to risk heroin's danger. The heroin-related death of Melvoin, or of other rock music icons such as Kurt Cobain, or Brad Nowell of the band Sublime, as well as heroin casualties of previous generations, such as Janis Joplin and Sid Vicious, now conjures a mystique of larger-than-life rebelliousness and recklessness for many young people, and compels them to use the drug in an effort to secure the same sort of celebrity immortality among their peers.

Heroin in the Media

Current attitudes toward heroin use also appear to have been influenced by the drug's portrayal in rock lyrics in recent years by idolized musicians who often have histories of heroin addiction themselves. The heavy-metal band Guns 'n' Roses, for example, enjoyed significant commercial success during the early 1990s with their single "Mr. Brownstone" (the title refers to the visual appearance of some heroin), and likewise, the decade ended with the commercially successful single "Heroin Girl" by grunge rock band Everclear. "Music lyrics have described and extolled the sensational experience of heroin," suggests Ginna Marston, vice president of Partnership for a Drug-Free America, "with poetic images of heroin, of opium poppies and 'getting low,' with band names mirroring the subculture of addiction, such as Morphine, Ammonia, and Jane's Addiction perpetuating the ethos and mystique of this drug."[32]

Resistance-training advocates note that since the early 1990s, the theme of heroin use has been treated not only in popular music, but also in several other areas of the media, and they believe that this has also significantly contributed to the social pressure to use the drug. They point, for example, to the numerous scenes of heroin use featured in movies throughout the 1990s. Notable among these films was *My Own Private Idaho,* in which then twenty-three-year-old actor River Phoenix depicted a hip, heroin-using, nomadic street hustler

Actor River Phoenix portrayed a heroin user in the film My Own Private Idaho, *and died of an overdose of heroin and cocaine, less than a year after the film's release.*

(Phoenix himself died of an overdose of heroin and cocaine within a year of the film's release), and *The Basketball Diaries* and *Pulp Fiction,* both of which rendered heroin as the "in" drug of the times.

The theme of heroin use was also seen in the world of high fashion when leading fashion photographer David Sorrenti created the "heroin chic" look in the mid-1990s. Sorrenti's photos of pale, anorexic, sunken-eyed models with blank stares took the fashion industry by storm, and even entered the realm of retail advertising in his Calvin Klein ads and Packard Bell computer commercials. In an effort to counter this glamorized portrayal of heroin use, the Partnership for a Drug-Free America began in 1996 to air TV commercials featuring grim images of real-life heroin addicts. When Sorrenti himself died in 1997 of a heroin overdose, President Bill Clinton criticized the fashion industry for compounding the heroin problem by glorifying heroin addiction for young people.

Reevaluating Resistance Training

For advocates of D.A.R.E. and other smaller resistance-training programs, the overwhelming scope and force of the pro-heroin messages recently seen in society underscore the desperate need for further development of resistance-training skills to protect young people. However, since the current heroin epidemic, as well as a significant rise in the use of synthetic stimulants and a number of other drugs, occurred after a decade of Project D.A.R.E. as the nation's primary prevention approach, doubts have emerged about the program. Critics of Project D.A.R.E.—some of whom were once staunch supporters of it—have begun to voice doubts about whether its resistance-training focus actually addresses the primary cause of drug abuse. A number of police departments that have taught Project D.A.R.E. in the nation's public schools have lost faith in the program's effectiveness, and have ended their involvement with it. Similarly, a number of the country's school districts have withdrawn from the program.

A number of studies conducted in recent years seem to support the observations of these schools and police departments about D.A.R.E.'s effectiveness. Among these is a study in which a group of one thousand ten-year-old students who were enrolled in D.A.R.E. classes were given a survey, and then, a decade later, they were given

President Clinton Denounces the "Heroin Chic" Fashion Trend

On May 21, 1997, a few days after the heroin overdose death of fashion photographer David Sorrenti, President Bill Clinton offered the following comments on the "heroin chic" fashion trend at a conference of United States mayors:

A lot of you have experienced in your communities the increasing allure of heroin among young people. We've seen a lot of communities where cocaine use goes down, heroin use comes up. For most people in our generation—a lot of you are younger than I am, but most of you are about my age—we all grew up thinking heroin was the worst thing in the world and there were these horrible images associated with it—strung-out junkies lying on street corners in decidedly unglamorous ways. But we now see in college campuses, in neighborhoods, heroin becoming increasingly the drug of choice. And we know that part of this has to do with the images that are finding their way to our young people.

In the press in recent days, we've seen reports that many of our fashion leaders are now admitting—and I honor them for doing this—they're admitting flat out that images projected in fashion photos in the last few years have made heroin addiction seem glamorous and sexy and cool. And if some of the people in those images start to die now, it's become obvious that that is not true. You do not need to glamorize addiction to sell clothes. And American fashion has been an enormous source of creativity and beauty and art and, frankly, economic prosperity for the United States, and we should all value and respect that. But the glorification of heroin is not creative, it's destructive; it's not beautiful, it is ugly. And this is not about art, it's about life and death. And glorifying death is not good for any society. And I hope that we have all come to recognize that now, because none of us are going to succeed unless all of us work together on this problem.

the same survey again. *Time* magazine reports, "The findings [of this study] were grim: 20-year-olds who'd had D.A.R.E. classes were no less likely to have smoked marijuana or cigarettes, drunk alcohol, used 'illicit' drugs like cocaine or heroin, or caved in to peer pressure than kids who'd never been exposed to D.A.R.E."[33] Similarly, a three-year study commissioned by the U.S. Department of Justice found that, though Project D.A.R.E. raises children's self-esteem, and improves their social skills and attitudes toward police, it has no measurable effect on drug abuse. Another criticism of the program is that its message to young people that they need to be

Students participate in Drug Abuse Resistance Education (D.A.R.E) day with former President George Bush in 1989.

vigilant—that dangerous drugs are everywhere—might actually lead them to try drugs in an effort to fit in.

In an attempt to reconcile their strong convictions about the dangers of social pressure with waning support for their program, the directors of Project D.A.R.E. have made significant changes to their curriculum, including a toning down of the urgency of its message about the danger of drugs. Other changes have included follow-up lessons at the seventh- and ninth-grade levels, as well as a switch to a group discussion format, rather than lecture-oriented lessons. Further, in response to the growing sentiment that drug abuse stems from a lack of satisfying alternatives to drugs, D.A.R.E. has begun to emphasize the importance of pursuing positive alternatives as part of its resistance-training curriculum.

The Alternatives Approach

New approaches to prevention are emerging because of the belief that resistance training—even with elements of other approaches added to it—does not address the root cause of drug abuse. One major approach claims that drug abuse is popular due to a lack of superior alternatives. The idea behind this approach is that young people become susceptible to the pressure to use drugs when they lack positive alternatives. "When asked to try heroin," author Jara Krivanek notes, "the perfect answer, of course, is another question: 'Why?' 'Why should I?' It is this stage that we should be aiming for. The ideal attitude of the citizen is to view heroin not as a predator waiting to pounce, but as an unimportant aspect of ordinary life that is not worth a second or even a first thought." [34]

Supporters of this "alternatives" approach to drug abuse prevention suggest that, rather than developing new methods of telling young people what not to be involved with, the estimated $700 million per year of government funds that are used for D.A.R.E. and other resistance-training programs would be better spent on programs that provide young people with the opportunity to participate in positive activities. Existing programs such as after-school sports, computer clubs, and community music ensembles are in dire need of additional funding, and many more such programs are needed to bring fun and satisfaction into young people's lives.

Parental Influence Approach

Another prevention approach that has gained support in recent years is frequently referred to as the "parental influence" prevention approach. This approach maintains that parents, rather than teachers or even uniformed police officers, hold the power to keep young people from using drugs.

Statistics show, however, that the majority of parents in the United States don't talk to their children about drugs. "Our greatest challenge," says Richard D. Bonnette, president of the Partnership for a Drug-Free America, "is helping all parents understand that they are a tremendous influence on their children's decisions." [35] Parental influence advocates suspect that parents do not discuss drugs with their children for a variety of reasons. Some parents, they suggest, still find it simply impossible that their children could become involved with drugs—at least not until they are "older." Others hesitate to discuss drugs with their children because they don't know what to say or how to say it. Still others are afraid of putting ideas into their children's heads.

In an effort to alert parents to the urgent need for their involvement in drug abuse prevention, Congress provided the Partnership for a Drug-Free America with an appropriation of $185 million in 1998 with which to create public service announcements. The resulting announcements have sought to inform parents that, as their children's first role models, their attitudes regarding drugs largely become those of their children. Thus, if parents don't seem to have a clear, unambiguous position on the matter of drug abuse, neither will their children, and this puts them at risk of trying drugs.

The Parental influence approach, therefore, emphasizes the need for parents to establish unambiguous rules for their children to follow regarding alcohol and other gateway drug use. The consequences of breaking these rules must be made clear, including what the punishment will be, how it will be carried out, how much time will be involved, and what the punishment is supposed to achieve. Further, parents must follow through with the described punishment if these rules are broken.

Parental influence advocates also advise parents to evaluate their own use of, and attitudes toward, tobacco, alcohol, prescription medicines, and even over-the-counter drugs, to become aware of the example that they are setting for their children regarding drug use. They do not believe that if parents are in the habit of having wine with dinner, for example, or an occasional beer or cocktail, they must stop. Children, they suggest, can understand and accept that there are differences between what adults may do legally and responsibly and what is appropriate and legal for children. They do suggest, however, that it is important for parents to keep this distinction clear for their children.

Combining Prevention Approaches

The Parental influence approach to drug abuse prevention also relies on the incorporation of other prevention approaches. For example, advocates of this approach believe that parents' prevention efforts that include an open, ongoing dialogue with children about drugs—particularly when it features straight talk—are quite helpful. Bonnette says, "Children who learn a lot about the risks of drugs at home are significantly less likely to try drugs—up to 50 percent less likely, according to our data."[36] Likewise, Parental influence advocates suggest that by forewarning children about the pressures that they may encounter to use drugs, as well as by providing them with plenty of positive alternatives to drugs, parents can further protect their children from the danger of heroin and other drugs.

Parents can help their children by educating themselves about drug use, including the paraphernalia used to take drugs.

The causes of heroin abuse have indeed proven to be numerous and complex. The Parental influence approach and other emerging prevention approaches may have the potential to eradicate the abuse of heroin and other drugs from society; however, the refinement of any prevention approach involves tremendous research and administration funds, and requires years of evaluation to gauge its effectiveness. Even after years of evaluation, it is difficult for researchers to determine with certainty the extent to which variables such as changing social trends have also come into play. Thus, since heroin abuse appears for the time being to be an inevitable problem in society, efforts to find effective heroin abuse prevention are best accompanied by effective programs for recovery from heroin addiction.

# Chapter 5

Recovering from Heroin Addiction

Before the 1960s, the only form of treatment available in the United States for heroin addiction was imprisonment in a federal correctional facility. Since there did not yet exist recovery programs to help end the cycle of heroin addiction, the only resource available to these addicts upon their release from prison was the support of their parole officers. Predictably, these addicts quickly returned to heroin use and its associated behaviors.

In recent decades, however, medical science has come to understand heroin addiction as a complex but treatable physical and mental illness, rather than a crime. Experts now know that with the proper treatment, people can and do recover from heroin addiction. They also understand quite well, however, that the recovery process is long and difficult.

Deciding to Recover

Most heroin addicts who have entered recovery programs found the resolve to do so only after having "hit bottom." An addict is said to have hit bottom when he or she arrives at the decision that life has grown unbearable because of drug addiction. Addicts can hit bottom due to any combination of the many physical and emotional

Heroin addicts enter a methadone clinic in New York. Methadone
maintenance programs help heroin users to recover from their addiction.

consequences of heroin addiction, and the depth to which an addict must sink before hitting bottom varies widely from one individual to the next. The less time it takes for an addict to hit bottom, the better the chances for recovering—not only because the consequences of heroin use will be minimized, but also because heroin addiction is considered a progressive illness, which means that the longer one remains addicted, the harder recovery becomes.

Substance abuse counselors sometimes use a technique called intervention to attempt to convince the addict to enter recovery before hitting bottom. The counselor, along with the addict's family, friends, and even coworkers, meet with the addict. In a loving and supportive way, the group asks the addict to honestly assess the negative effects of his or her addiction. If the addict consents to entering recovery, the counselor makes the necessary arrangements. Very often, however, the addict feels attacked and betrayed by intervention efforts, which are effective only a small percentage of the time.

Though heroin addicts arrive at the decision to enter recovery under a variety of circumstances and for a variety of reasons, they must all begin the recovery process with a common first step, which is detoxification from the drug. The experience of detoxification is one with which all heroin addicts are already familiar to some extent, since they experience the beginnings of it every time the effects of the drug wear off and withdrawal symptoms begin to occur. When addicts undergo detoxification without the aid of medications to ease their discomfort—an experience addicts often refer to as "going cold turkey"—withdrawal symptoms reach peak severity about twenty-four hours following termination of drug use, and can continue at this level for up to a week or more.

Free Heroin Clinics

During the years preceding the time when heroin was made illegal in the United States in 1924, in an effort to curtail heroin addiction, public health officials took the controversial step of opening forty clinics across the United States where addicts could go to obtain free heroin. The doctors who operated the clinics suggested that they improved addicts' health, since one condition for receiving the free drug was that addicts had to undergo medical examinations and treatment. Critics note, however, that many people tried heroin for the first time at these clinics, and that the program inadvertently raised the number of addicts in the country.

In 1998, the World Health Organization (WHO) conducted clinical trials in Geneva, Switzerland, to determine whether the practice of providing heroin to addicts in a clinical environment was a useful solution for the problem of addicts who refused methadone. The initial findings of the WHO committee suggested that free heroin clinics provided a number of benefits to society, including reduced crime, and heightened public interest and awareness on the issue of heroin addiction. Further benefits, they suggested, lay in the program's requirements that addicts forfeit their driver's licenses and receive frequent health screenings as a condition for participation in the program. These conditions, they found, protected the safety and health of the general public, and saved millions of dollars in medical expenses. Based on these findings, research facilities in the United States, including Johns Hopkins University, began to investigate the possibility of conducting similar clinical trials.

Though intensely unpleasant, unless severe health problems already exist, the detoxification process is not ordinarily life threatening.

To avoid the withdrawal symptoms that accompany detoxification, addicts entering recovery may elect to take medication to either prevent these symptoms or lessen their severity. The most commonly used drug for this purpose is methadone. Methadone, which is administered orally and given in decreasing doses over a seven-to ten-day period, can provide a relatively symptom-free detoxification. A drawback of using methadone for detoxification is the fact that methadone itself is addictive, and causes withdrawal symptoms of its own when the addict discontinues its use. Its symptoms are milder than those of heroin, however, and can themselves be lessened with other medications.

Other medications used to ease heroin withdrawal are nonaddictive. Clonidine, for example, which was originally a blood pressure medication, has been found to be a helpful alternative to methadone for those who do not wish to create a new drug dependence. While not as effective as methadone in suppressing muscle and joint aches, clonidine does provide significant relief for the anxiety, chills, running nose, and stomach cramps of withdrawal. Withdrawal symptoms can also be treated individually as needed with over-the-counter remedies such as ibuprofen.

Inpatient Treatment Programs

Many addicts may undergo detoxification on an outpatient basis, living at home but reporting to a hospital, drug clinic, or doctor's office daily to receive both withdrawal medication and counseling. Most substance abuse counselors believe, however, that it is preferable to undergo detoxification in an inpatient treatment program, in which addicts live for a prolonged period of time in an addiction treatment facility and undergo withdrawal under constant professional supervision. One obvious benefit of detoxifying in an inpatient facility is that the addict does not have access to heroin. Another benefit is the fact that the addict receives the constant support and encouragement of counselors, most of whom are recovering addicts themselves, and is surrounded by other

The Haight Ashbury Free Clinic in San Francisco uses the "therapeutic community" approach to treating drug addiction.

detoxifying addicts who are also embarking on the long journey to recovery.

Most inpatient facilities use the "therapeutic community" approach, which combines the cold turkey approach with group therapy and support from other recovering addicts. "This is chemical cold turkey," note the directors of the Haight Ashbury Free Clinic in San Francisco, "but the community usually maintains a high level of support to counter withdrawal and to create a healing atmosphere for aftercare and recovery." [37] Life in a therapeutic community also usually includes daily participation in group therapy sessions, in which addicts voice and examine their feelings with the help of fellow addicts. Some therapeutic communities cater to specific groups of heroin addicts. For example, there are programs that allow women to live with their children, to help them learn responsible parenting skills. Many facilities also prepare addicts for employment, and provide other skills that are helpful for reentry into society.

Successfully completing detoxification, even in a rigorous inpatient program, is merely the first step involved in recovery, however, and it offers no guarantee that the addict will remain clean. "Heroin addicts" states the *New York Times*, "are notoriously resistant to permanent recovery. More than 80 percent of addicts who manage to withdraw from heroin eventually go back to it."[38] Though the addict's physical dependency on the drug may have been broken, mental and emotional dependency can still be severe indeed, and can cause repeated relapses.

Treating heroin addiction, explains author Margaret O. Hyde, "can be as demanding of patience as the curing of cancer."[39] Regardless of the time period in which an addict has abstained from using heroin, tolerance never returns back to zero, and it reaches high levels far more quickly in a relapsing addict than it does in beginning heroin users. Thus, the relapsing addict soon needs large amounts of the drug to stay high.

In recent years, Academy Award–winning actor Robert Downey Jr. has demonstrated for the American public how overwhelming the temptation of heroin can be for a recovering addict—even for one who has completed numerous inpatient treatment programs, as

Actor Robert Downey Jr., a prominent heroin addict, leaves court after being arraigned on drug charges.

Acupuncture

Acupuncture, which has been used by physicians for thousands of years in the Far East, is gaining widespread acceptance in the West for the treatment of heroin addiction. Based on the ancient Chinese therapeutic practice of inserting very fine needles in key nerve centers, acupuncture treatment for heroin addicts was pioneered by Dr. Michael Smith at New York City's Lincoln Hospital in 1972, where he found that it provides heroin addicts with significant relief from the symptoms of withdrawal, as well as the "junk hunger" that can make long-term recovery difficult. Daily acupuncture sessions have since been shown to lower the dropout rates in detox centers significantly. Though researchers do not yet understand how acupuncture achieves these results, they suspect that the needles stimulate the brain's production of endorphins and other neurotransmitters.

well as jail sentences, for drug use. "It's like I have a loaded gun in my mouth and my finger's on the trigger," Downey told a judge during a court appearance for drug charges in 1999. "And I like the taste of the gunmetal."[40]

The kind of overwhelming cravings experienced by recovering heroin addicts seem to be quite different from those experienced by addicts of other drugs. Referred to as "junk hunger," these cravings are often described by addicts as a strong feeling of sadness combined with a physical sensation of emptiness within the abdomen. Though researchers know that junk hunger is the result of one or more of the various permanent chemical and physical changes that take place within the heroin addict's brain and body, they do not yet know the exact cause of junk hunger. Nor do they know why some recovering addicts experience it to a far greater degree than others. The Do It Now Foundation explains that whatever its cause, "learning to handle recurrent flashes of junk-hunger is something that a good many ex-junkies get to handle for the rest of their lives. But considering the alternative, most think it's not a bad trade-off."[41]

Lifelong Methadone Maintenance

For hundreds of thousands of addicts who wish to recover but are unable to withstand the craving for heroin, help is available through

Methadone patients, pictured here, experience fewer withdrawal symptoms than most recovering heroin addicts.

methadone maintenance programs. In addition to preventing withdrawal symptoms during an addict's detoxification, daily oral doses of methadone can also provide ongoing relief for the addict's heroin cravings without creating any intoxicating effects, and without the need for increases in dosage. Also, methadone actually blocks the effects of heroin, so that the addict will not get high if he or she does take the drug. So long as the treatment schedule is followed, a methadone maintenance patient will be a normally functioning, alert, and healthy person. A thirty-seven-year-old housewife in Brooklyn, for example, says this of her experience with methadone maintenance:

> I began using drugs when I was twelve. By the time I was sixteen I was shooting heroin, living in the street, really down and out. I've been on methadone since I was twenty, and it's kept me on the road. If it hadn't been for the program I'd be dead. Now I'm on the board of the PTA at my daughter's elementary school. I go shopping, take care of the house, love my family—my life looks as normal as anyone else's. No one knows I'm on methadone, not even my daughter.[42]

Among the benefits to society of methadone maintenance programs is a steep reduction in the crime rate among the addict community, as well as a slowing of the spread of AIDS and other communicable diseases because of the reduced number of intravenous heroin users. Despite these significant benefits to individuals as well as to society, however, some recovery experts object to the practice, suggesting that heroin addicts can and must achieve sobriety without the aid of medications to fully recover from their addiction.

While the topic of methadone maintenance is hotly disputed, there is widespread agreement in the recovery community that there is a significant difference between simply living clean and actually recovering from the emotional damages of heroin addiction. "Many heroin addicts," explains Margaret O. Hyde, "have . . . emotional problems or character disorders before they become addicts. Even if they do not, their life develops into one in which they lie, cheat, and steal in order to get the drugs that they need."[43] Thus, many addicts struggle with painful feelings such as guilt, shame, and inferiority upon getting clean. Making matters worse, addicts usually come out of addiction at about the same stage of emotional development at which they entered it. Even valuable insights and positive attitudes learned during extended inpatient treatment programs can fade from memory with the passing of time, leaving the addict at the mercy of despair, and therefore in danger of returning to drug use.

Support Groups for Addicts

In an effort to keep from returning to heroin use, as well as to recover emotionally from heroin addiction, many recovering addicts join support groups. The largest by far of these groups, Narcotics Anonymous (NA), is modeled after the highly successful alcoholic support group, Alcoholics Anonymous. NA and similar support groups call themselves "twelve-step" groups because they employ the Twelve Step Program of Recovery used by Alcoholics Anonymous. This program's twelve steps outline the actions that addicts need to take to recover from addiction.

One of the many ways that the twelve steps help addicts to recover is by requiring them to acknowledge to themselves and another person all of the people that they harmed on account of their addiction, and to then set about making amends with those people if possible. Many addicts find that this step eases their conscience tremendously and therefore makes the idea of remaining clean seem less daunting. Another emotional need is met by a step that requires the addict to attempt to help other addicts in their recovery process. In addition to curtailing the self-centeredness that is so characteristic of addicts, this step provides the addict with a new sense of purpose in life, and a meaningful alternative to being high. "The idea of one addict helping another," notes Anthony Kiedis of this effective as-

The Twelve Steps of Narcotics Anonymous

The following are the 12 Steps of Narcotics Anonymous. These steps, which were adapted from the 12 steps of Alcoholics Anonymous, summarize Narcotics Anonymous's program of recovery from addiction.

1. We admitted that we were powerless over our addiction, that our lives had become unmanageable.

2. We came to believe that a Power greater than ourselves could restore us to sanity.

3. We made a decision to turn our will and our lives over to the care of God as we understood Him.

4. We made a searching and fearless moral inventory of ourselves.

5. We admitted to God, to ourselves, and to another human being the exact nature of our wrongs.

6. We were entirely ready to have God remove all these defects of character.

7. We humbly asked Him to remove our shortcomings.

8. We made a list of all persons we had harmed, and became willing to make amends to them all.

9. We made direct amends to such people wherever possible, except when to do so would injure them or others.

10. We continued to take personal inventory and when we were wrong promptly admitted it.

11. We sought through prayer and meditation to improve our conscious contact with God as we understood Him, praying only for knowledge of His will for us and the power to carry that out.

12. Having had a spiritual awakening as a result of these steps, we tried to carry this message to addicts, and to practice these principles in all our affairs.

Anthony Kiedis, lead singer of the band Red Hot Chili Peppers, has found the support of fellow recovering addicts to be instrumental to his own recovery from heroin addiction.

pect of twelve-step recovery, "there is nothing that touches that as far as I'm concerned."[44]

Also common to most twelve-step programs is a spiritual element—a belief that addicts must rely on their individual understanding of God for the strength and wisdom to remain clean. Although not every recovering addict believes in God, the directors of the Haight Ashbury Free Clinic in San Francisco suggest that the twelve-step approach can work for any addict, regardless of his or her views on religion:

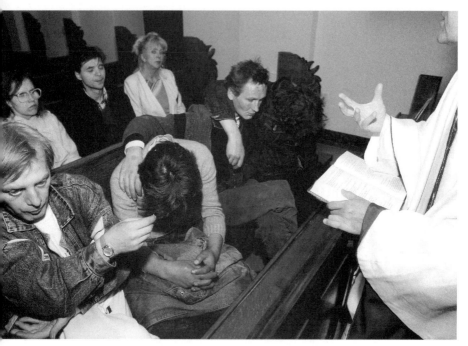

Many recovering addicts prefer support groups which feature a strong spiritual component. There is a wide variety of support groups available, including those that do not emphasize spirituality.

In truth, there are many chapters of AA and other self-help programs that do have a decided religious bent. On the basis of this and the many references to God and prayer in the twelve steps, some people have accused the self-help movement as a whole of being in some way related to the fundamentalist Christian movement. It is not. But those who cannot accept these aspects of a program should not categorically reject all self-help groups. There are meetings of self-help programs for agnostics, atheists and even secular humanists. These programs will definitely take a different interpretation of "God as we understood Him," which is fine. [45]

In addition to twelve-step and other kinds of secular addict support groups, other chapters of these organizations target specific groups of addicts, such as those infected with the HIV virus. Thus, while it is doubtlessly true that no particular support group suits all addicts, the wide variety of recovery support groups available makes it extremely likely that any recovering addict can find a suitable group.

Support Groups for the Addict's Loved Ones

Additional support groups exist for the families and friends of addicts, and their participation in these groups can actually assist in the recovery of the addict. The most prominent of these groups is Nar-Anon, which is also based on the twelve steps of Alcoholics Anonymous. Having usually spent years worried and agonizing over how to persuade their loved one to quit using heroin, people often turn to organizations such as Nar-Anon expecting to learn how to get their addict into a recovery program, or to ensure that their recovering addict remains clean. These people are often surprised, therefore, to hear that the most they can do to aid in their addict's recovery is to heal their own emotional problems—that they themselves are in need of a recovery program for the emotional damage that heroin addiction has had on their lives.

Loved ones of addicts have often developed an irrational, obsessive sense of personal responsibility for the addict's habit, recovery, and overall well-being. Often referred to as "codependency," this sense of responsibility can lessen the addict's sense of personal responsibility for his or her actions and addiction. Further, the obsession of codependency can affect virtually all areas of a codependent person's life, and can lead to a wide range of destructive and compulsive behaviors, such as workaholism and overeating. Also, codependency often leads to a wide range of stress-related illnesses, including migraine headaches, ulcers and other stomach problems, high blood pressure, depression, anxiety, insomnia, and even hyperactivity.

Thus, though often initially alarming for newcomers to programs such as Nar-Anon, the knowledge that they are powerless to prevent their addict's use of heroin can become a great source of relief. And, ironically, when addicts detect emotional detachment and recovery in their loved ones, they are themselves often unburdened of much of the guilt that can make it more difficult to become or remain clean. In this way, an addict's loved ones can significantly assist in the addict's recovery, though not in the way that they might have assumed.

Increased understanding of the complex emotional obstacles to effective recovery from heroin addiction is leading to even more comprehensive recovery programs. In the meantime, though still difficult, long-term recovery from heroin addiction can actually be a joyful experience for addicts. James W. West of the Betty Ford Center states this of the process of recovery from heroin addiction:

> From sadness, isolation, and despair, many emerge through recovery to reach greater heights than if they had not fallen. Life in recovery is a mix of gratitude and serenity. People speak of an aura of wonderment as they experience an intense freedom from being sick in such an unpredictable, compulsive, and tragically self-destructive way. Life in recovery also brings loving and still hesitantly hopeful dear ones and friends back into reach. There is a humility that arises from the awareness of the depth of the illness from which revered persons arise. There is deep thankfulness to those who stuck with them. Coping with inevitable hard and even tragic times is part of . . . strong recovery. Eventually there comes that positive attitude that is so necessary to being a helper rather than a victim in society to which one now truly belongs and functions effectively.[46]

Thus, the fact that recovery from heroin addiction is such a long and difficult process is not viewed by all recovering addicts as a burden. In comparison to the period in which they were using heroin, during which they may well have felt as if they were in the process of dying, recovery brings many addicts the sense that they are in the constant state of becoming something more than they were the day before—that they have never felt so alive.

Notes

Chapter 1: The Origins of Heroin

1. Dr. J. C. D. Wells, "Poppy Juice and Willow Bark: Advances in Their Use for the Twenty-First Century," The Pain Web. www.thepainweb.com/doclib/topics/000009.htm.
2. Quoted in Mary E. O'Brien, M.D., "Overpowering Pain: A Serious Problem Comes Out of the Closet," *Postgraduate Medicine*, vol. 102, no. 1, July 1997. www.postgradmed.com/issues/1997/07_97/obrien.htm
3. Michael A. E. Ramsay, M.D., "Anesthesia and Pain Management at Baylor University Medical Center," *Baylor University Medical Center Proceedings 2000*, vol. 13, pp. 151–65. www.baylorhealth.com/proceedings/13_2/13_2_ramsay.htm.
4. Charles F. Levinthal, *Messengers of Paradise: Opiates and the Brain*. New York: Anchor Press/Doubleday, 1988, p. 21.
5. Levinthal, *Messengers of Paradise*, p. 20.
6. Quoted in Levinthal, *Messengers of Paradise*, p. 21.
7. Alfred W. McCoy, *The Politics of Heroin in Southeast Asia*. New York: Harper & Row, 1972, p. 3.

Chapter 2: Heroin Abuse in the United States

8. U.S. Department of Justice, Drug Enforcement Administration, Heroin. D.O.J. Los Angeles Division, 1986, p. 5.
9. McCoy, *The Politics of Heroin in Southeast Asia*, p. 17.
10. McCoy, *The Politics of Heroin in Southeast Asia*, p. 6.
11. Jara A. Krivanek, *Heroin: Myths and Reality*. Boston: Allen & Unwin, 1988, p. 61.
12. Margaret O. Hyde, *Mind Drugs*, 4th ed. New York: McGraw-Hill, 1981, pp. 27–28.

13. Hyde, *Mind Drugs,* pp. 27–28.
14. Hyde, *Mind Drugs,* p. 30.
15. U.S. Department of Justice website, "Heroin." www.usdoj.gov/dea/concern/heroin.htm.
16. Quoted in Robert Mathias, "NIDA Conference Aims 'Preemptive Strike' at Increased Heroin Use Among Nation's Young People," *National Institute on Drug Abuse Notes,* vol. 12, no. 6, November/December 1997, p. 5.

Chapter 3: Consequences of Heroin Addiction

17. Jim Parker, "Heroin: The Junk Equation," Do It Now Foundation, June 2000. www.doitnow.org/pages/105.html.
18. Mathias, "NIDA Conference," p. 5.
19. Quoted in Parker, "Heroin: The Junk Equation."
20. Quoted in U.S. Department of Justice, *Heroin,* Committee on Government Reform and Oversight, House of Representatives, 104th Cong., 2d sess., Washington, D.C.: U.S. Government Printing Office, 1997, p. 33.
21. Mathias, "NIDA Conference," p. 7.
22. James W. West, *The Betty Ford Center Book of Answers.* New York: Pocket Books, 1997, p. 106.
23. Quoted in U.S. Department of Justice, *Heroin,* p. 33.
24. Quoted in Krivanek, *Heroin: Myths and Reality,* p. 56.
25. Quoted in David Dodd, *Playing It Straight.* Deerfield Beach, FL: Health Communications, 1996, p. 77.
26. Quoted in Dodd, *Playing It Straight,* p. 88.
27. Quoted in Krivanek, *Heroin: Myths and Reality,* p. 76.
28. Quoted in U.S. Department of Justice, *Heroin,* p. 21.

Chapter 4: Preventing Heroin Abuse

29. Richard Seymour and David E. Smith, M.D., *DrugFree: A Unique, Positive Approach to Staying Off Alcohol and Other Drugs.* New York: Facts On File Publications, 1987, p. 26.
30. Quoted in U.S. Department of Justice, *Heroin,* p. 82.
31. Mathea Falcon, *The Making of a Drug Free America,* New York: Random House, 1992, p. 33.

32. Quoted in U.S. Department of Justice, *Heroin*, p. 42.
33. Reaves, "Just Say No to D.A.R.E.," *Time*, February 15, 2001. www.time.com/time/education/article/0,8599,99564,00.html.
34. Krivanek, *Heroin: Myths and Reality*, p. 246.
35. Quoted in "More Parents Talking with Kids About Drugs More Often, and Appear to Be Having an Impact," Partnership for a Drug-Free America. www.partnershipforadrugfreeamerica. org/NewsCenter/pats/pats1.asp?ws=PDFA&vol=1&grp=News Center&cat=National+Surveys&top=Articles&Pyear=1999+ Parents&Pname=pats199x.asp&pNum=7.
36. Quoted in "More Parents Talking with Kids About Drugs More Often."

Chapter 5: Recovering from Heroin Addiction

37. Seymour and Smith, *DrugFree*, p. 81.
38. Mary Duenwald, "A Fresh Look at a Quick Fix for Heroin Addiction," *New York Times*, December 4, 2001. www.nytimes.com/ 2001/12/04/health/psychology/04DETO.html?ex=100850 0993&ei=1&en=0d46d0eaa71ad61d.
39. Hyde, *Mind Drugs*, p. 83.
40. Quoted in Reaves, "Will Robert Downey Jr.'s Case Spark a Change in Drug Sentencing?" *Time*. www.time.com/time/nation/ article/0,8599,98373,00.html.
41. Parker, "Heroin: The Junk Equation."
42. Quoted in Falcon, *The Making of a Drug Free America*, p. 127.
43. Hyde, *Mind Drugs*, p. 83.
44. Quoted in Dodd, *Playing It Straight*, p. 93.
45. Seymour and Smith, *DrugFree*, p. 108.
46. West, *The Betty Ford Center Book of Answers*, p. 197.

Appendix:
Warning Signs of Heroin Abuse

While the following warning signs are not positive proof of heroin abuse, and can be indications of other drug, health, or personal problems, together these changes form a pattern frequently associated with heroin abuse.

Behavior Associated with Heroin Use

Continual wearing of long-sleeved garments, particularly in hot weather, or reluctance to wear short-sleeved attire when appropriate.

Wearing of sunglasses at inappropriate times.

Unexplained loss of money or possessions.

Unusual borrowing of money from friends, coworkers, or parents.

Stealing small items from work, home, or school.

Increasing and inappropriate anger, hostility, and irritability.

Deterioration in relationships with friends and family.

Evasiveness when asked about new friends.

Withdrawal from responsibility, including abrupt changes in work or school attendance, quality of work, work output, grades, and discipline.

Decreased interest in hobbies.

Deterioration of physical appearance, grooming, and hygiene.

Secretive behavior regarding actions.

Hostility in discussing the topic of drug use.

Physical Warning Signs Associated with Heroin Use:

Scars (tracks) on inner arms or other parts of body from needle injections.

Red, cracked, or raw nasal passages from snorting heroin in powder form.

Weight loss.
Constricted pupils that fail to respond to light.
Lethargy or drowsiness.
Difficulty in concentration.
Euphoria.
Slurred speech.
Nausea, vomiting, and other flulike symptoms.

Organizations
to Contact

The following organizations provide a wide variety of information about heroin, including where to find treatment and support groups for heroin addicts. Local phone books generally list service referral and hot-line numbers for these services in each state.

Do It Now Foundation
Box 27568
Tempe, AZ 85285-7568
(480) 736-0599
www.doitnow.org

A nonprofit publisher of substance abuse literature. Its target audiences include middle school, high school, and college students and their families.

Heroin-Information.org
www.heroin-information.org/heroin/pages/rehab_options.html

Contains links to the web pages of over seventy-five heroin treatment centers in the United States.

Nar-Anon Family Group Headquarters, Inc.
P.O. Box 2562
Palos Verdes Peninsula, CA 90274
(310) 547-5800

A nonprofit self-help fellowship whose purpose is to support the family and friends of drug abusers.

Narcotics Anonymous (NA)
PO Box 9999
Van Nuys, CA 91409
(818) 773-9999
www.na.org

A nonprofit self-help organization that provides a recovery process and support network for those addicted to heroin and other narcotics. Members share their successes and challenges in overcoming active addiction and living drug-free, productive lives through application of the principles contained within the twelve steps and twelve traditions of NA.

**National Clearinghouse for Alcohol and
Drug Information (NCADI)**
11426-28 Rockville Pike, Suite 200
Rockville, MD 20852
(800) 729-6686
www.health.org

Drug information specialists are available to provide the most current and comprehensive information about substance abuse prevention and treatment.

**National Council on Alcoholism and Drug
Dependence (NCADD)**
20 Exchange Place, Suite 2902
New York, NY 10005
(212) 269-7797
Twenty-four-hour affiliate referral: (800) NCA-CALL
www.ncadd.org

Provides information on prevention, intervention, and treatment, and seeks to reduce the stigma of alcoholism and other drug addictions.

planet-know.net
www.planet-know.net/first.htm

A website which provides information for teens about the abuse
and psychoactive effects of heroin and other drugs.

Glossary

acquired immunodeficiency syndrome (AIDS): An incurable and fatal disease of the body's immune system; the viral agent, HIV, can be sexually transmitted, or can be obtained through the sharing of drug needles.

addiction: A chronic, relapsing disease, characterized by compulsive drug seeking and use, and by chemical and molecular changes in the brain.

clean: The condition of being "drug-free."

craving: A powerful, often uncontrollable desire.

detoxification: A process allowing the body to rid itself of a drug; often the first step in a drug treatment program.

fentanyl: A heroin analog that can be more than 50 times more potent than heroin.

hepatitis: An inflammation of the liver, which can be contracted through the sharing of drug needles.

methadone: A long-acting synthetic medication shown to be effective in treating heroin addiction.

Narcotics Anonymous: A self-help support program for drug addicts that includes meetings that follow the twelve-step recovery plan.

outpatient: A patient who visits a clinic or hospital but does not stay the night.

physical dependence: An adaptive physiological state that occurs with regular drug use and results in a withdrawal syndrome if use of the drug is stopped; usually occurs with tolerance.

rehabilitation: Being in a state of recovery, as from drug addiction.

relapse: The return of a person in a recovery program to drug use or drinking.

tolerance: A condition in which higher doses of a drug are required to produce the same effect as during initial use; often leads to physical dependence.

toxic: Poisonous.

withdrawal: Physical and emotional symptoms that develop when an individual is physically addicted to a substance, and levels of that substance begin to drop in the body.

For Further Reading

Books

Dr. Neil Beck, *Beating Heroin*. New York: Putnam Books, 2000. Contains essential information for heroin addicts as well as their loved ones, and discusses approaches to the recovery process.

Martin Booth, *Opium: A History*. New York: Simon & Schuster, 1996. Provides an in-depth look at the impact that opium has had on human history.

Sean Covey, *The Seven Habits of Highly Effective Teens: The Ultimate Teenage Success Guide*. New York: Simon & Schuster 1998. Provides a step-by-step guide to help teens meet such challenges as avoiding peer pressure–based decisions, building friendships, achieving their goals, and getting along with their parents.

Barbara Hughes, *Drug Related Diseases*. New York: Franklin Watts, 1987. Gives in-depth information on the diseases associated with the various forms of drug abuse.

Wendy Mass, *Teen Drug Abuse*. San Diego: Lucent Books, 1997. Discusses the various drugs abused by teens, and examines the startling rise in teen drug use in recent years.

Gerald G. May, M.D. *Addiction and Grace: Love and Spirituality in the Healing of Addictions*. Harper San Francisco, 1988. Discusses the role of spirituality emphasized in most drug recovery programs.

Robert O'Brien, and Sidney Cohen, *The Encyclopedia of Drug Abuse*, 2d ed. New York: Facts On File, 1992. Provides comprehensive information on a wide range of drug abuse subjects.

Internet

Teen Challenge World Wide Network, "A Parent's Guide on Drug Abuse." www.teenchallenge.com. Presents a wide range of information to help parents prevent their children from abusing drugs.

Works Consulted

Books

The Big Book of Narcotics Anonymous, 5th ed. Los Angeles: Narcotics Anonymous World Service Office, 1988. Outlines the "twelve steps," the "twelve traditions," and other central features of the Narcotics Anonymous recovery program.

David Dodd, *Playing It Straight.* Deerfield Beach, FL: Health Communications, 1996. Features essays written by numerous actors, musicians, and other celebrities about their recovery from drug addiction or alcoholism.

Mathea Falcon, *The Making of a Drug Free America.* New York: Random House, 1992. Analyzes the effectiveness of America's drug abuse prevention and drug addiction treatment programs.

Margaret O. Hyde, *Mind Drugs,* 4th ed. New York: McGraw-Hill, 1981. Provides an informative overview of commonly abused drugs, both legal and illegal.

Jara A. Krivanek, *Heroin: Myths and Reality.* Boston: Allen & Unwin, 1988. Examines the various treatment and prevention methods used for heroin abuse in the United States and Australia.

Charles F. Levinthal, *Messengers of Paradise: Opiates and the Brain.* New York: Anchor Press/Doubleday, 1988. Discusses recent breakthroughs in understanding the way the human brain works, including how heroin affects brain chemistry.

Alfred W. McCoy, *The Politics of Heroin in Southeast Asia.* New York: Harper & Row, 1972. Examines the opium and heroin trade in Southeast Asia prior to 1972.

Richard Seymour and David E. Smith, M.D., *DrugFree: A Unique, Positive Approach to Staying Off Alcohol and Other Drugs.* New York: Facts On File Publications, 1987. A wide range of valuable information on recovery from drug addiction is offered by the directors of the Haight Ashbury Free Clinic in San Francisco.

U.S. Department of Justice, Heroin, Committee on Government Reform and Oversight, House of Representatives, 104th Cong., 2d sess., Washington, D.C.: U.S. Government Printing Office, 1997. Various public health experts testify before Congress concerning the current heroin epidemic.

U.S. Department of Justice, Drug Enforcement Administration, Heroin. D.O.J. Los Angeles Division, 1986. Provides a comprehensive overview of heroin, including its origins and use, as well as the legislative attempts to prevent its use in the United States.

James W. West, *The Betty Ford Center Book of Answers*. New York: Pocket Books, 1997. The director of the Betty Ford Center for the treatment of drug addiction responds to commonly asked questions about a wide range of drug-related subjects.

Periodicals

Robert Mathias, "NIDA Conference Aims 'Preemptive Strike' at Increased Heroin Use Among Nation's Young People," *National Institute on Drug Abuse Notes*, vol. 12, no. 6, November/December 1997.

Internet

Bill Clinton, "Remarks by the President at U.S. Conference of Mayors, May 21, 1997." www.drugs.indiana.edu/prevention/clinton.html. Provides the transcript of a speech in which President Clinton discusses the resurgence of heroin use in the United States and criticizes the fashion industry for glamorizing the use of heroin.

Doctor's Guide Online, "Long-Term Heroin Addicts Have Only 50 Percent Survival Rate, Thirty-Three-Year Study Finds." www.pslgroup.com/dg/1fb4aa.htm. Article discusses the findings of a thirty-three-year research project conducted by the University of California at Los Angeles on the health consequences of long-term heroin addiction.

Mary Duenwald, "A Fresh Look at a Quick Fix for Heroin Addiction," *New York Times*, December 4, 2001. www.nytimes.com/2001/12/04/health/psychology/04DETO.html?ex=10085009

93&ei=1&en=0d46d0eaa71ad61d. Discusses a controversial method procedure in which heroin addicts undergo rapid detoxification while under sedation.

Geocities.com, "Geopium Opium Throughout History." www.geo cities.com/CapitolHill/Senate/5428/opiumhistory.html. Provides a detailed chronology of opium's long history, and lists books for further reading on opium and heroin.

Mary E. O'Brien, M.D., "Overpowering Pain: A Serious Problem Comes Out of the Closet," *Postgraduate Medicine,* vol. 102, no. 1, July 1997. www.postgradmed.com/issues/1997/07_97/obrien. htm. Provides an extensive discussion of the various anesthetics used throughout history.

Jim Parker, "Heroin: The Junk Equation," Do It Now Foundation, June 2000. www.doitnow.org/pages/105.html. Provides an overview of the history, manufacturing process, chemical effects, abuse, and dangers of heroin.

Partnership for a Drug-Free America, "More Parents Talking with Kids About Drugs More Often, and Appear to Be Having an Impact." www.partnershipforadrugfreeamerica.org/News Center/pats/pats1.asp?ws=PDFA&vol=1&grp=NewsCenter& cat=National+Surveys&top=Articles&Pyear=1999+Parents&P name=pats199x.asp&pNum=7. Discusses the need for parents to be responsible for their children's avoidance of drugs, and provides methods for parents to use.

Michael A. E. Ramsay, M.D., "Anesthesia and Pain Management at Baylor University Medical Center," *Baylor University Medical Center Proceedings 2000,* vol. 13. www.baylorhealth.com/ proceedings/13_2/13_2_ramsay.htm. Discusses the use of opium as one of the first surgical anesthetics and provides a detailed history of anesthesia.

Jessica Reaves, "Just Say No to D.A.R.E.," *Time,* February 15, 2001. www.time.com/time/education/article/0,8599,99564,00.html. Discusses the efforts of Project D.A.R.E.'s directors to improve the effectiveness of their drug abuse prevention curriculum.

———, "Will Robert Downey Jr.'s Case Spark a Change in Drug Sentencing?" *Time.* www.time.com/time/nation/article/0,8599, 98373,00.html. Actor Robert Downey Jr.'s high-profile drug abuse treatments and drug-related jail sentences are used to consider America's approach to the drug problem.

Substance Abuse and Mental Health Services Administration, "Heroin Snorting on the Rise." www.drugabusestatistics.samhsa. gov. Provides a wide range of statistics related to drug abuse in the United States.

United States Department of Justice, "Heroin." www.usdoj. gov/dea/concern/heroin.htm. Provides a useful overview of the pharmacology, trafficking, and abuse of heroin in the United States.

Dr. J. C. D. Wells, "Poppy Juice and Willow Bark: Advances in Their Use for the Twenty-First Century," The Pain Web. www.the painweb.com/doclib/topics/000009.htm. Provides a substantial review of the medicinal use of willow bark and opiates throughout history, as well as a brief discussion of the responsible use of these substances in modern medicine.

Carter M. Yang, "'An Old Heroin Town' One in Ten Residents of Baltimore Is Addicted to Heroin." *ABCNews*, March 14, 2001. www.abcnews.go.com/sections/us/DailyNews/heroin010314_ balitmore.html. Discusses the current heroin epidemic in Baltimore, Maryland.

Index

acupuncture, 81
addiction
  babies suffering from, 54–55
  crimes connected to, 30–31
  criminalization of, 29, 75
  death caused by, 49
  desensitization caused by,
    54–55
  diseases related to, 49–52
  immaturity resulting from,
    52–56
  inner city and, 29–31, 34
  inpatient treatment for,
    78–81
  medical problems related to,
    42, 44–56
  mental illness resulting from,
    52–56
  physical, 46–49
  power of, 10, 27–28
  prostitution and, 32
  psychological, 52–56
  rock musicians and, 52–53,
    55, 56, 65–67, 84–85
  see also detoxification; with-
    drawal
additives, 44–45
advertisements, 68
Aerosmith, 52–53
AIDS, 50, 55
Alcoholics Anonymous, 83, 87

alternatives, to drug abuse, 71
American Medical Association,
  23
Avicenna, 15

babies, 54–55
Baltimore, Maryland, 38
Bayer Pharmaceutical Com-
  pany, 23–24, 25
Betty Ford Center, 50, 88
Bonnette, Richard D., 71–72
brain, 46–48
brand names, 65
Burroughs, William S., 46

cartels, 39–41
celebrities, 65–68
Centers for Disease Control
  and Prevention, 50
central nervous system, 46–48
Civil War, 22
clinics, dispensing free heroin,
  29–30, 77
Clinton, Bill, 68, 69
clonidine, 78
Cobain, Kurt, 55–56, 66
cocaine
  cartels and, 39–41
  glamorization of, 38
  history of, 6
  side effects of, 7

codependency, 87
"cold turkey," 77–78
  see also detoxification
Colombia, 39–40
coping skills, 52–56
cough suppressant, 26–27
crime, 36, 54, 57
crime syndicates, 32–33

depressant effect, 44
desensitization, 54–55
designer heroin, 46
detoxification, 77–78, 79–80
diacetylmorphine, 24
diseases, 49–52, 57
Do It Now Foundation, 45, 81
Downey, Robert, Jr., 81–82
Dreser, Heinrich, 23–24, 27
Drug Abuse Education Act of
  1970, 61–63
Drug Abuse Research Center, 49
drug cartels, 39–41
Drug Enforcement Administration, 30, 41
*DrugFree: A Unique, Positive
  Approach to Staying Off Alcohol
  and Other Drugs* (Seymour
  and David E. Smith), 62
drug testing, 37

Egyptians, 12–13
endorphins, 47–48
Everclear (rock band), 67

Falcon, Mathea, 60–61
Federal Bureau of Narcotics,
  60
fentanyl, 46
Ford, Betty, 50
French Connection, the, 33

Galen, 14
gangsters, 31–33
gateway drugs, 59
glamorization, 38, 65–69
"going cold turkey," 77–78
  see also detoxification
"Golden Crescent," 33
"Golden Triangle," 32, 36
Great Depression, 34
Greeks, 13–14
Guns 'n' Roses (rock band),
  66–67

Haight Ashbury Free Clinic,
  58, 79, 85–86
Harrison Narcotic Act, 20, 27
hepatitis, 50
"heroin chic," 68
Heroin: Myths and Reality (Krivanek), 54
heroin smoking, 41
Hippocrates, 14
"hitting bottom," 75–76
HIV, 55
Homer, 14
Hyde, Margaret O., 36,
  37–38, 80, 83
hypodermic needles. *See* needles

Iliad (Homer), 14
illegalization, 29
illness concept, 75
immigrants, 35
inner city heroin usage, 29–31,
  34
inpatient treatment, 78–81
intervention, 76

Johns Hopkins University,
  46–47, 49, 77

Joplin, Janis, 66
"Just Say No" campaign, 64, 65

Kelen, Gabor D., 49, 51, 57
Kiedis, Anthony, 53, 84–85
Krivanek, Jara A., 35, 54

laudanum, 17–18, 22
Leshner, Alan, 42
Levinthal, Charles F., 22
"lines," 41
liver, 50, 51
Love, Courtney, 56
Lucchese, Thomas ("Three
    Finger Brown"), 33
Luciano, Salvatore C.
    ("Lucky"), 31–33, 34

Mafia, 31–33, 34
Marcus Aurelius (emperor of
    Rome), 15
marijuana, 7, 60–61
Marston, Ginna, 67
McCaffrey, Barry, 59
McCoy, Alfred W., 23, 32–33,
    34
media, 15, 66–68
medical problems, 42
Melvoin, Jonathan, 65–66
mental illness, 52–56
meperidine, 46
Mesopotamia, 12
methadone, 78, 81–83
Mexico, 43
middle class, 36
misinformation, 59–61, 62
morphine, 6, 18–20
movies, 66–67
musicians. See rock bands

names, 24, 25
Nar-Anon, 87
Narcotics Anonymous (NA),
    83–84
National Institute on Drug
    Abuse (NIDA), 42, 43, 46
needles, 19–20, 50–52
neurons, 47
nicknames, 42
nicotine, 7
NIDA. See National Institute
    on Drug Abuse
1970s, 38
1960s, 36–37
Nirvana (rock band), 55
Nixon, Richard M., 37
Nowell, Brad, 66
number of addicts in United
    States, 43
    see also statistics

Office of National Drug Con-
    trol Policy, 59
opium
    ancient beliefs about, 8
    Civil War and, 22
    discovery of, as first pain rem-
        edy, 12
    endorphins and, 48
    history of, 11–23
    in 19th-century medicines,
        21–22
    overdose and, 15
    as poison, 14–15
    poppy growing, 25
    smoking of, 16–18, 22
    tea made from, 11–12
opium pipe, 16
opium poppy, 11, 25

Opium War, 17
origins, 11–23
Osler, William, 20
overdose, 44, 65–66, 68

Paracelsus, 17–18
parents, 71–72
Partnership for a Drug-Free
  America, 67, 68, 71–72
peer pressure, 63, 65–66
Phoenix, River, 67–68
Pliny the Elder, 14
poison, 44–45
pregnancy, 54–55
prevention, 58–74
Project D.A.R.E. (Drug Abuse
  Resistance Education), 65,
  68–71
Project S.M.A.R.T. (Self-Man-
  agement and Resistance
  Training), 63–64, 65
prostitution, 32
Pure Food and Drug Act, 27

Ramsay, Michael A.E., 18
Reagan, Nancy, 64
receptor sites, 47
recovery, from addiction,
  75–88
Red Hot Chili Peppers (rock
  band), 53
Reefer Madness (film), 60–61
resistance training, 63–65, 68–71
respiratory illnesses, 24–25, 26–27
respiratory system, 44
rock bands, 52–53, 55, 56,
  65–67, 84–85

SAMHSA. *See* Substance

Abuse and Mental Health
  Services Administration
self-esteem, 63, 69
Sertuerner, Friedrich, 18
Seventies, the. *See* 1970s
sexually transmitted diseases, 51
Seymour, Richard, 62
SIDS (sudden infant death
  syndrome), 55
Sixties, the. *See* 1960s
Smashing Pumpkins, The
  (rock band), 65
Smith, David E., 62
Smith, Michael, 81
smoking. *See* heroin smoking;
  marijuana; nicotine; opium
smuggling, 39
snorting, 41
social consequences, 57
social pressure, 65–66
Sorrenti, David, 68, 69
Southeast Asia, 39–40, 63
  see also "Golden Triangle"
Special Action Office for Drug
  Abuse Prevention, 37
statistics, 43, 49, 50, 68–69, 80
steroids, 6
straight talk, 61–63
Sublime (rock band), 66
Substance Abuse and Mental
  Health Services Administration (SAMHSA), 42
suicide, 55–56
Sumerians, 12
support groups, 83–88
syndicates, 43
synthetic heroin, 46

teenagers, 36, 42

testing, 37
therapeutic communities,
  78–81
tobacco, 16
tuberculosis, 50
  see also respiratory illnesses
Twelve Step Program of Recovery, 83–84
Tyler, Steven, 52

urbanization, 29–31

Valium, 6
venereal disease, 51

Vicious, Sid, 66
Vietnam War, 36
violence, 57

war on drugs, 37–38
Wells, J.C.D., 12
West, James W., 50–51, 88
withdrawal, 46
  see also detoxification
Witherspoon, John, 22–23
World Health Organization,
  77
World War II, 34–35
Wright, C.R., 24

Picture Credits

Cover Photo: Associated Press, AP
AFP/CORBIS, 59
Bettmann/CORBIS, 9, 19, 23, 31, 33, 37, 45, 64, 70, 76, 82
CORBIS, 21, 26, 53
Henry Diltz/CORBIS, 66
Robert Holmes/CORBIS, 79
Hulton/Archive by Getty Images, 14, 15, 16, 30, 35, 47, 50
Ed Kashi/CORBIS, 56, 86
Kobal, 60, 67
Buddy Mays/CORBIS, 32
Brandy Noon, 48
PhotoDisc, 41
Reuters NewMedia Inc./CORBIS, 40, 80
S.I.N./CORBIS, 55, 85
Ted Streshinsky/CORBIS, 73
Michael S. Yamashita/CORBIS, 13

About the Author

Todd Howard holds a master of arts degree in English literature from California State University, Long Beach. He is a freelance writer and editor, and has taught English at both the elementary school and college levels.